Heaven Now!

A Child's Journal of Dreams

Rachel Christiana with Mama G

1

HEAVEN NOW!

Thelma Goszleth

lougoszleth@hotmail.com

Ordering Information:

Quantity sales. Special discounts are available on quantity purchases. For details, contact the publisher.

Published through

info@ilncenter.com

Five Stones Publishing

"I was in Heaven. Angels didn't take me.

I was just there! People told me to wait until I got to Heaven.

I said, "NO, I'm going to have Heaven on earth."

Musings From Mom

Rachel is my daughter. In many ways she is an average eleven year old. She loves wearing long dresses and having her nails painted. She really doesn't like cleaning, and she doesn't always feel like doing her school work. Yet, Rachel is also my best prayer partner.

If you want to capture Rachel's attention, start talking about Heaven, someone to pray for, or a miracle and she is all ears. She will give her attention for hours. It is like you are finally speaking her language.

It wasn't always like this. Although I believed babies and children were quite tuned into the spirit world, that didn't seem to be true for Rachel. She often was afraid when she was little. I sometimes had to sit up nights with her. She didn't have nightmares, the fear was when she was awake.

I started asking her if she had any dreams when she was three or four. Around four or five, she began remembering her dreams.

One evening she ran to Grandma's room afraid again. In bed with Grandma they talked about looking at Jesus instead of the scary things. Soon she surprised Grandma, by going back to her own bed! And, she slept all night.

When we asked her about it in the morning, she said, "When I looked at Jesus I saw Him". That sentence blew me away, so simple yet so profound. What you focus on is what you see and what you live out of.

From that time until now she has continued to dream of Heaven and angels, Jesus, God, and the Holy Spirit. It has been an answer to my prayers in so many ways, and I am often in awe.

When my daughter, who has a limited imagination and is always truthful, tells me things about Jesus, the Alone Room or the History Room in Heaven, I am again overwhelmed by God's grace. He has given me a window to look through. Although I look forward to more of my own experiences, I know I have truly been given a gift.

One morning during a stressful time, I was still in bed worrying and planning when Rachel came to tell me her dream. It was the one where she is an adult in her dream, and she is at a Heaven waterslide. She can slide as many times as she wants, but she only does it once a week—because she is too busy.

The angels say, "What are you doing!?" in a way that means, "Are you crazy?"

I knew it was loud and clear for me! "Lighten up! Don't worry! Enjoy life! I've got it!"

So, is Rachel special? Absolutely! She is sweet, beautiful, loving, and pays attention to what Heaven is speaking.

Is every other person on earth, including the children, special?

Rachel will be quick to tell you, "Absolutely!" We can all hear, see, and experience Heaven everyday if we will just look.

In Rachel's words "It is not far." Heaven is closer than the air we breathe. Just look at Jesus. I promise you will see Him.

With this book I am sharing one of my greatest treasures. Enjoy!

Hi, I'm Annika. I'm the one that thot of the frunt of the book, and Aunt June painted it. Well Heaven is a WonderFul Plaec. It's a Plaec where people open up to see God.

I see visions sometimes. They are wonnerful. In fact they are amazing.

I like to write notes. And, I made the angel for Mama's Little People story book.

LOVE FROM JESUS!

Heaven is for now!

And, it's all about Jesus!

He is LOVE!

Always!

So, we begin with some 'sneak peeks' of extra special times with Jesus, taken from this journal. These peeks may seem short and simple; but in reality, they are very long and very deep.

These precious moments seem 'too holy' to write for all to read. Yet, they are exactly what Jesus wants Rachel to share. And, she shares gladly, with a heart that yearns for everyone to know how much they are loved.

This is her mission. —Mama G—

EXCERPTS:

July 2013. .Then I didn't ask anything else, but I just looked at Him; and, He looked at me for the rest of the dream. I don't know what that means, but I think it is because we are one. He is in me, and I am in Him.

In a lot of dreams. . that happens—that we just look at each other. And I haven't known what it means. But I think it is because we are in each other, and we are each other.

. .We ended up in the Love Room. Jesus wasn't in the room with me, but I felt His Love all around me. It was a great feeling! After a few minutes, I went out. I asked Jesus, "How much do you love me? I know you love me, but how much?"

He said, "As much as the stars."

That's just as an example. But He explained what He meant—"More than you can count! More than you can know!"

I have tried to count it in my head, and I can't. He meant it's more than I can know now, and also more than I can handle. I would just fall down on the floor and not be able to get up.

January 27, 2013. . I was in heaven, standing right next to Jesus. He was crying, and saying, "I love you, Daughter." He was leaning down holding my hand and walking with me.

"Why are you leaning down?"

"Because I am so happy for you. . to show you my Love." In a half crying way, He said, "Come with me, Daughter."

We went to a room that was outside. I don't know what it was called. There was no door. The room was very high, and had like a deep ditch. He asked, "Do you want to slide down?"

"But it's impossible to slide down a mountain!" I was crying myself—just in His Love more than ever before—down on my knees. "Thank you, Jesus. Thank you, Jesus." I crawled up to Him and touched His knees, crying beside Him. *(This was with deep feeling, not usually expressed by Rachel.)*

He lifted His cloak, and under it was His blood. "Oh, it should be gone by now!" I said. It was on His knees, and His feet.

But He said, "It won't be gone until everyone in the whole entire world knows My Love, how much I love."

Thoughts from Mama, the Scribe

As I journal for Rachel, I am overwhelmed with amazement and appreciation for God's gifts to us—'Little Guides' leading the way into another dimension reality. Jesus said we need to become like a child to enter the Kingdom realm. How often I give thanks for Rachel, leading our family into heaven awareness, the Heaven that is touching earth NOW!

From the time she was very small, Rachel was a realist, not known for good imagination. We know quite well what she knows. So, it has become very clear that she is experiencing, seeing, and hearing beyond anything she has learned on earth, or imagined.

Her mother started journaling for her when she realized this was more real than just sweet dreams—to keep for Rachel—for when she grew up. As the dreams increased, I became her scribe.

She came into my room morning after morning in recent months, ready to relate her night visit to Heavenly realms. She closed the door, so there would be no distractions. Scribbling as fast as I could, I was often in awe and wonder. I felt the importance of just being her scribe, letting her use her own words. And, I often was amazed at the words she used that weren't really in her vocabulary. Also, amused at other words and descriptions that are not in my vocabulary!

We became a team, as she slowed to my pace, and repeated word for word whenever I got behind. She is very precise about her conversations with Jesus.

As the dream visits increased, there were times I was away. But, she was not worried at all. When we got together again, she could recall in vivid detail all the night visits while I was away—in order, day by day.

Eventually, we realized Rachel was not given just to our family, to lead us into the heavenlies. But, her experiences were meant to be shared, for anyone who was searching for the High Places. She has been very, very happy that we write for her, knowing that it is for others. And, as Jesus told her, it will encourage people around the world! Rachel now has her own sense of urgency to get this good news out.

This is not a book to be read at one sitting. It is a journal of many visits to Heaven, taken over a period of several years.

Glimpses of many precious moments of a child, hand-in-hand with her Heavenly Father and Friend. Moments too precious to be scrutinized or explained.

But gladly shared, so that somebody will be encouraged.

So, read a little. Then, close your eyes. Look and listen. Experience Heaven for yourself as you tip toe through this journal.

It is with great joy we share this precious treasure.

2007 and 2009
Age Five to Six

Rachel's Heaven journeys began before she could journal, or understand very much. She had a special book she used for pictures of Heavenly things she saw, or experienced. Many pictures were without explanations.

When we became aware that Rachel was having so many dream visits to Heavenly places, we began to journal for her, in her special book in her own words. Some of her early pictures are scattered throughout this journal.

DECEMBER 9

There were three angels and three chairs, purple and pink. I saw Jesus sitting on his throne, a deep red-purple chair. He said to come sit on His lap. I did. There were baby angels and big angels in my room. I held the big angel's hand and we went up to Heaven.

A week later I was in Heaven. There were three chairs for angels, and a red chair for Jesus. I wanted to sit on the angel's lap. I did.

Another night I saw a green imp that made me afraid. I went to Mama's room. We talked about just looking at what Jesus was doing, and at the angels. I went back to my room by myself. When I just thought about Jesus and angels, I saw them, and had good dreams about them.

This was a 'breakthrough' for Rachel—from the many night scares and coming to sleep with Mommy or Mama, needing someone to pray with her and stay with her. She was seven, and just beginning to recognize the difference between the night 'voices' that caused fear, and God's Love that brings peace and safety.

Once, I dreamed Granny and Papa came to visit from Heaven. It was a very short visit. They said, "Hi," and looked around the house, looking for my dad. They left, and then I kept singing a song.

Baby angels flying

God is so wonderful!
God is so wonderful!
Jesus, You're my Helper.
Angels, you're His helpers.
Oh Heavenly Father (4x)
You're so wonderful!

Another time, when I was alone at home, and awake, the angels came (Daddy was home, but I was alone). I saw this like a picture. They helped watch me, so I wasn't afraid. They went and brought a locket from Heaven. It had verses:

For God so loved the world. . .
There is no fear in Love. .
I am crucified with Christ. .
Jesus is in my heart now!
Jesus is in my heart now!

I dreamed that I was nine years old, and I was in Art School. There were other children there, who believed in God, but not in Jesus.

(Do you think they were Jewish?) "Yes."

One little boy dreamed about Jesus, and started to love Him. Jesus told me the Jewish children won't stay Jewish, because of their dreams. Three children got to know Jesus—all the way. They had Joy Dreams every night.

Another December night, I dreamed a lot of people were at our house. A big Rachel and a lot of men. Big Rachel had two little babies that were twins. They were one, and could walk, but not talk. They said 'La – la," when they liked something, and waved. One was a girl, and one was a boy. Their names were Baby Flower, and Baby Book, because that is what they liked. They always waved at them (flowers and books), and said, "La – la".

13

In my first dream about this, we were putting names on the doors where people were staying. I kept writing 'Little Rachel.' This upset Big Rachel, and she kept changing it to say, 'Big Rachel'. She had the same twins in my first dream.

And, another—We were on a walk. I kept saying, "Where are we going?" We were at a place where there was nothing. I didn't know where we were going. We lived in a different country on our road. I didn't like it because it smelled like gas outside, and fire inside our house.

On our walk, we had gone on a perfect road. (It smelled perfect.) At first I didn't understand why it smelled like gas outside. Then I knew it was because people were pouring gas on the road. They weren't thinking right.

And our house smelled like fire because people visiting had little things with fire inside. To me, this wasn't good.

At the end of my dream, I knew why the people were pouring gas on our road, and bringing fire. It was because the President said they had to. If they didn't, he would take all the money away.

At the end I was sad for some people because they didn't obey this mean president, and he took ALL their money. They didn't even have a penny. On this road, some people were happy and some sad. The white people were happy. The black people were sad.

On the perfect road, the President of this country was thinking right. They didn't pour gas anywhere. It smelled perfect. Some people on this road were happy, some were sad, and some were sleepy.

2010
Age Seven

MAY

I was almost going into a place where I would be stuck (by believing lies), but Jesus helped me stop going in there. Other people were in there. There was a fence and a motel. They were stuck by believing Satan's lies.

Then I came to a gate. Some people were trying to go over or around the gate, but it didn't work. I went through it. Annika did too, and she went somewhere else.

I went into a big room. There was a rainbow, but it was a bad rainbow—the wrong color. I didn't like it, so I left to find Annika. I found her on a path sitting on a bench outside. I thought it was Heaven until God told me it was "Heaven on earth."

We then went into a building where babies were worshipping. I thought it was strange that babies were singing. But then I found out they were angels. They were hiding their wings, so Annika wouldn't be afraid.

When Mommy said that sounded silly, I said, "It is not silly! It is just true."

MAY 6

I was walking but then I stopped, because I knew I was going to fall. Then God told me, "Keep walking. Don't stop. You will not fall in."

Then He told me to jump off the bridge. The water in my dream wasn't just normal water. It was healing water. Then I understood why He wanted me to jump in it. I did jump in.

May 9

I was at home, then I was going somewhere. But I didn't know where I was going. At first God didn't tell me where, but He told me to go. It was a place only for me. It had a lot of birds.

God told me to look for something. I didn't know what. Then I found a bottle of water. I didn't want to drink it because I thought it wouldn't taste good. It had been there a long time. Then God told me to drink it. When I drank it, I could feel it healing my teeth.

Then I saw Jesus. I had a penny in my hand. Jesus told me to give it to a man who believed in Jesus. He told me he was a disciple from the New Testament. Then He said we are all His disciples. When I gave it to him Jesus gave me a lot of money—big ones and small ones.

May 10

In my dream, I was littler than I am now. I saw a plant God had made. It wasn't a flower. And after I saw it, I heard just one bird tweet.

PICTURE DREAM

I was with Jesus in the grass having a picnic. I see eating the picnic as eating His Words for my soul. We eat His words for our soul by speaking them. I saw a picture of my teeth healed—especially the one that is black, that is loose. It wasn't black anymore.

A VISION

I was standing, looking at a framed picture of myself when I was three. I knew I was three and my teeth were perfect, and my nose smelled perfect—because Jesus was standing beside me and told me.

Jesus and Annika were beside me in the framed picture. I think Jesus was showing me that He was fixing my teeth and Annika's too. Why did I see a picture of Annika?

JUNE 14

I was in Heaven. Angels didn't take me. I was just there! People told me to wait until I got to Heaven. I said "NO, I'm going to have Heaven on earth."

Rachel's Mom—I prayed before bed that the girls would experience Heaven all night. Interesting that she was just there—without angels taking her there. This became a strong statement that we keep coming back to. We began realizing we do have that choice, though many of us have not known we do.

JULY 5

I wasn't flying. I was on the ground looking at the stars. One looked very BIG. I thought it was God reminding me how big He is.

JULY 6

I saw a gift from Jesus. I thought that inside must be healing for my teeth. Jesus said how to open the gift is to say the truth, and sing songs.

JULY 8 – PICTURE DREAM

I saw myself singing to people. But, then, Jesus told me I wasn't singing. I was talking—telling my testimony. It was my testimony of my teeth being healed. *(This was something we prayed for every night.)*

JULY 14

I was alone in my dream, and I didn't know Jesus. He came to me and wanted to show me His friends. They were his disciples.

In the end, I knew Him and He went back to Heaven. So, I was feeling how orphans feel, and how they meet Him.

AUGUST 9

I was going somewhere with God, but I didn't know where. He first took me to a fountain. The water splashed on my hands. It tickled, and made me laugh.

Then we went to a place. I didn't know if it was a store or what. It had a lot of food and drinks. This place represents everything you need.

Then on the way, we stopped at a waterfall. This water was healing water. We came to two paths—a long one and a short one. The long one was made of sand. The short one was made of rock. This is like the foolish man and the wise man. We took the short rock path and it took me to the secret place.

August

I was home, but then I was just somewhere else. I didn't know how I was somewhere else. I wasn't even walking or anything. I realized angels were flying me there. It felt like it.

I didn't know where I was going. There was a path with a few jewels. When I got to the place, there were a lot of jewels. On the path I got a ring that was shaped like a 'C' that was closed. It had a round stone that was red with white in the middle.

Jesus was with me in the beginning of the dream. Jesus told me He died on the cross for me. I thought it was strange, because I already knew that. Then I realized it was for me to tell others.

August

I was walking. I saw a little girl. She was living at a house that was only big enough for her. She knew there was a God, but she was told He was bad, and Jesus was bad. I told her that wasn't true. Then God told her He was good. Then she believed and was very happy.

SEPTEMBER 14

At the beginning of my dream, demons came and tried to trick me. They tried a lot of things, but it didn't work. Then I felt an angel beside me. I didn't see it, but I knew the angel was there.

The demons tried again, but it didn't work because the angel was there.

> *"Jesus told me He died on the cross for me. I thought it was strange, because I already knew that. Then I realized it was for me to tell others."*

UNDATED

I was in a little playhouse. It had room for two people. A lot of kids started coming in. I said, "There isn't enough room!"

When I came out, there was a lot of children that didn't have houses. All they could do was sit and cry. They didn't know Jesus. . had parents but were like orphans.

I told them about Jesus, and they listened, except one child that only listened to his parents. I thought I could tell his parents the truth. Then he would listen to them.

I think playhouse re ' sents (re-pre-sents) surprises from God!

2012
Age Eight

MAY

Rachel came running into my room one morning.

"Mama, Mama! I saw your Mom!"

"You saw her?! From here? Or were you there?" I asked in surprise.

"When I am in Heaven, I am there. And she was taking care of babies in Heaven. Not the real little ones that were in mommies's tummies—who didn't want them, and got them out. The angels take care of those. But she was taking care of ones like Sammy and Roc, two or three years old."

"Oh, Rachel! That's wonderful! Did you tell her who you were? But of course she would know."

"No, I was too shy. When I'm in Heaven, I mostly just talk to the angels."

"So, Rachel, tell me what she looked like."

"Her clothes were real sparkly! Her hair was dark and curly."

What an awesome wave of God's Love for me—to send me an "update", a glimpse of Mom through my grand-daughter. My mom died the year before Rachel was born. As I thought about this surprise glimpse of Mom's eternal 'ministry', I wasn't surprised that she was still 'mothering'. And I began to tell Rachel what a wonderful mother, and grandmother she was, and how she 'mothered' little children on many missions to Haiti. I told her about the little black rag doll that I had just seen again at Dad's house. Mom had made lots of them to give to the little girls.

"Yes, Rachel, Grandma did have very black, very curly hair when she was younger. Grampa always said she was the prettiest girl on campus!"

AUGUST

I was rocking back and forth like I do in Heaven to worship. It wasn't doing what it does in Heaven. I was only seeing things in my room.

There was a quiet knock at the door and it was my angel Laughy. I wondered why the knock was so quiet. Laughy said because human knocking sounds louder.

I held hands with Laughy and went to Heaven. I was in a room and heard angels singing very quiet. I wondered why they were quiet because mostly the angels are pretty loud when they sing in Heaven.

I thought I had been in this room before because I was looking down at earth. But I asked why it was so quiet. They said it was The Quiet Room, and that I hadn't been here in this way before (a lot of rooms in Heaven look down on earth).

I saw toys, block creations, etc., and stuff that I had made on earth. I was told that this is the room you come to when you have quiet times on earth. But in the day you just see pictures of things (like what will happen tomorrow).

However, at night in my dreams I got to see the room from Heaven's perspective. At the end I joined the angels singing. Then it was time to come back to earth and I woke up.

Another time I was exploring Heaven by myself. I then looked for Jesus and angels. They were in the quiet room and sang this song. "In Heaven there is always fun." Heaven doesn't have names of songs because the song is its own name.

There was a circle of white and orange spinning fire, like the whirlwind that took the angels to Heaven. It disguises as fire and turns into white. Why? Jesus said some things in Heaven can't be seen the same on earth (the fire can only be seen in Heaven).

August

I was in Heaven looking down on earth. I saw some people crying. It was a family that had been rear-ended in a car accident (the father didn't check in the rear view mirror). They (two girls and the parents) were crying beside the car, because there was a three-year-old dead in the car. They would not leave the car or let anyone take the baby. They were praying for a miracle but nothing was happening (they didn't believe in Jesus. They were Muslim).

I then came to earth. I prayed. I didn't really say anything. I just touched the little girl and she came to life. I then told the family their baby was alive, but they didn't believe me. Even when they saw her, they thought it must be another baby. They took her to the doctor, and he said she couldn't be the same baby. Then, they looked her over very closely, and knew it was their baby. When they realized it was her, they believed in Jesus!

I was in Heaven because they were going to show me the next building. The name of the building was God's Promises. I went into the room. There was a picture of Noah and the ark with a rainbow. The picture wasn't colored. When you touched the picture it became colored.

It took a while. After it was colored you could touch it and go inside the picture. Only Noah was in the picture. When I went inside I looked like his wife. I was just in there a little bit. Then angels brought me out.

Heaven waterslide. It was a waterfall. I only went down it a few times, although I could do it all I wanted. I was grown up and too busy working. I just did it like once a week, like on the week end (days off).

Angels in Heaven said, "What are you doing?! You should be doing this a lot!" It was the water of life—refreshing and fun.

I said, "Rach, that one is definitely for me—for all of us grown-ups!" What an indictment—'grown up and too busy working' ! ! !

Rachel told about her recent visits to the History room and her new angel Lovely. Lovely often walks with her, or they ride horses to Heavenly places. Other angels usually fly, sometimes taking her hand and flying her there with them. In the History Room, she goes back in time and sees 'stories' as they are happening.

One time, she saw a lot of people listening to Jesus, and they didn't want the children to bother Jesus. Then Jesus called them to come around Him.

Another time, she saw a girl ask Jesus to heal her son. He followed her, and when He saw her son, He touched him and he was healed. There were many other times, and many stories from the Bible.

She told about a short dream of seeing orphans whose friends were sick. Rachel came and said, "They are not sick; they are just pretending—like Jesus said about the little girl." Then she prayed for them and they were healed.

Rachel said that many nights the dream is over before she wakes up and then Jesus comes and talks to her about the dream or other things. She said when he tells her something special, it is an extra happy day.

2012
Age Nine

JANUARY

I was in my room rocking in a big rocking chair. I was listening to music. I heard music outside my room with words. I opened the door and a lot of angels were there. All the angels I knew plus some more I didn't know yet, but I knew they were all my angels. I had seen them before in The Quiet Room.

Invisible Star and Crystal talked to me. They told me that they were here to teach me the other angels' names, and for them to learn my language. They told me one angel's name was Gold. I said "What? That is a color."

They said, "Yes, colors are Heaven names."

Another angel was named Blonde. I asked Invisible Star why her wings looked like they were cut in half.

She said, "I really do have big wings but it helps me turn into a waterfall. Would you like a party?"

I knew she meant a dance party. At the dance party she was talking in a Heaven language. It sounded like music. Then she sang in English. I had not heard the song before.

Then the white big circle thing came to take them home. I said "Goodbye Invisible Star!" and then I saw Laughy. She was there the whole time, but I didn't see her until then.

In my dream, I ran downstairs and told my mom and dad all about it. I said "I can't believe I saw that!"

MAY

The History Room and discussions about the nearness of Heaven.

Sometimes you just go through the roof and you are there. And, yes, rooms and houses sometimes look just like here so you can't always tell where you are."

One night, the angel Crystal said, "Instead of the History Room, we'll see the Surprising Room!"

I saw (giggle)—it was sort of funny—funny animals in Heaven, dancing around. They were different colors like a child would color, part one color and 'patches' of other colors!

They were small and medium sizes, but not like animals we have on earth. There was a stage. There weren't other people there. Only angels were with me, if they needed to answer my questions. The angels were surprised too, because it is always different. And they can go there sometimes to see what is happening.

JULY

I was exploring by myself in Heaven. I did not see Jesus or angels. I went into the Finding Room. There was a hidden door that led to the stables. It was a shortcut. Angels were also hiding in the room, my angels and great grandma's.

I decided to go through the door, and look for the angels later. The room nearby is called The Alone Room. You can walk or you can ride the horses.

So I rode a horse to the Alone Room. I saw Jesus. It was a room to be alone with Jesus without all the people and angels. It was a little. . pretty.

There was a place to sit if you wanted to sit down. The room was sparkly white and purple. I sat and talked with Jesus. He told me things I didn't know before.

Jesus gave me a necklace. Jesus told me this necklace is for whenever anyone has to go somewhere. It was like a locket. Jesus said, "Open it." It had stories and verses from the Bible. It was gold, and had a picture of Jesus on the front.

On earth it is called a locket. In Heaven, it is called a keeper of your favorite stories and verses. You can call things whatever you want in Heaven. No one minds.

Jesus said, "When you know your favorite verses—when you think of them, they will come into the necklace.

I told Jesus, "Thank you so much!" Then I left. It was the end of the dream.

Jesus told me: "You can come to this room whenever you want."

I asked, "Why are things prettier in Heaven, but it looks like earth?"

Jesus said, "Because it is to show the beauty of Heaven, but also that you are always in Heaven."

I have like a jewelry box—very pretty. It is where I keep my special things. I called it my Jesus Keeper—to keep stuff He gives me, all my favorite stuff. I could call it what I wanted!

September Sunday in the Philippines

Rachel had been wanting to go on a mission with us (Mom and Dad) to the Philippines garbage dump and orphan ministry. It was not an easy trip, but we knew it was God's plan for Rachel. We wondered if she would experience some kind of healing. She didn't have any specific diagnosis, but had challenges that we knew she should not have to live with.

She did very well in the whole experience. One day she had this 'encounter' after spending the morning sick. Her tummy was hurting, and she had not eaten. But, she had to go somewhere with us. As we were riding in the car, she suddenly lifted her head and looked up, smiling. Here is her experience.

First I was hearing angels singing, "Oh how I love you! Oh how I love Him!" over and over. When I looked up, I saw Jesus and the angels. And, always, behind the angels are white sparkles. And all the rooms of Heaven were behind them because all different parts of Heaven were coming out at different times.

Then I saw this waterfall from way above coming down into me. I call it the 'Fix Waterfall' because it fixed half of my mind.

Then I heard Jesus whisper. When He whispered, it wasn't like a quiet whisper. It wasn't as quiet as normal—more like talking. They call it a whisper in Heaven. Maybe because the angels are really, really loud when they are singing!

I have heard Him whisper it before. But He said, "I love you a whole lot!" And, the other half of my mind was fixed.

I used to be afraid, because I only thought He loved me a very little. All my fear was taken away. It used to be like—I thought things were chasing me, or going to steal me, or eat me. It was all just in my mind. It wasn't real. But now that is all gone.

The doors in Heaven were all open. For just a moment it was like I went up and saw Heaven coming down to earth.

Rachel was immediately healed. Her frown turned to a smile. She was in awe. She was so amazed that this happened during the day, not when she was dreaming. We soon were at a restaurant, and she ate three pieces of pizza! She could hear the song, and join in singing for a long time after. Since then she has talked quite a bit about the waterfall healing her mind.

OCTOBER 8 A DREAM VISIT TO AN ORPHANAGE IN AFRICA

I went to help them. I had a place where I hid some money, my secret money place. I gave the lady who cares for them three dollars, and she put it in her pocket. Later she discovered lots of money in her pocket! A miracle!!!

The lady was like African American. She spoke English and another language too. So we started talking. She said, "This isn't true." She didn't believe in God. She didn't believe anything she couldn't see with her eyes.

I said, "Did you ever close your eyes to see Him?"

She said, "Yes, but I didn't see anything." She told me her mother, who she trusted more than her dad, didn't believe in God at all. Her dad believed in God, but thought He wasn't really good.

I asked, "Why did you start this job in the first place?--to care for so many kids?"

She said she couldn't have any children, so she did this.

"God can give you a child." I said.

"There isn't a God."

Then I told her maybe she should stop this job for a while, and go tell her family the truth.

So, she did go tell her parents they were wrong. And told her family that she could have her own children. Her parents didn't agree with her. But she said, "The truth is the truth. You'll have to find out for yourselves!"

Then she showed them the money in her pocket, enough for all the orphans. So she told them it was God who gave it.

Then they started to believe! God told me He was talking to her while I was talking to her, so she was beginning to believe!

OCTOBER 15

I was in Heaven waiting for the angels before going exploring. They had told me the night before that they had something to show SPECIAL!

for tomorrow night. But they said 'next day' because of course it's always day!

So when Laughy and Lovely came, I said, "Why are you late?"

They said, "We're not late. It's never late in Heaven!"

They went to the Jewel Room, which was pretty, not because of the room, but because of Me! I was there by myself, knowing I was beautiful like a jewel. And, that everybody that goes there is the same. Jesus sees them the same way.

The angels waited outside, which they only ever did before at the Alone Room. Then we walked to the Heavenly Ballroom!

Once I got up to Jesus, I said, "I know You are here. . but, what is this room for?"

He said, "When I come to get all of you, I will bring you to this room and marry you!"

Ever since I was in Heaven, I have wondered where that would be. It was so amazing, I fell down! That's what you do in Heaven when you are amazed and excited!

It is the most beautiful room I have seen in Heaven..the walls..the glory..and no chairs, because nobody sits and watches! Jesus said, "The angels will be standing all around the edges. And, you will know everybody's angels."

This is the first time He has told me anything about the future—in Heaven. The truth is, He doesn't even know when it will be. His Father knows, and He will tell Him.

I did ask Him, and I was surprised He didn't know. He said, "My Father even has surprises for Me! And for His little children."

We all know He's going to come back, but He doesn't know when.

Some of the angels were bridesmaids, dancing with us. And something like flowers there—that weren't flowers.

So I ended up—I woke up—still in the room alone with Jesus. I still feel that I am there. I always know I am there, even when I can't feel that. My mind says it's night, but I know it's always day. So it's like a second morning! And it isn't because of my Philippine trip.

OCTOBER 19

I was in the Love Room. I would call it the Presence Room because His Love flows out of His Presence. Sparkly white stuff comes down—into your whole body.

Angels called for me. They needed me in a certain spot. I felt so excited whenever I was close to the Presence—in the rooms, more than outside.

The waterfall is like that too—exciting like the love flow. Some water falls are very small—like just dripping out of a crack.

The Presence Room and Surprise Room changes from one time to another..new things are added.

Next to it, two rooms together called The Future Room. It shows things in the future. Things were not very clear. But when you stay awhile—because you want to know—then you will see more.

I saw that America in the future will always be a free country. Every time you go, you will see more.

Then I went to the Alone Room. Jesus gave me a ring. It was the ring I will have at the wedding. I said, "But it is many years before the Wedding!"

He laughed, "All will get them long before the wedding. This is more than just any wedding ring! It has many 'showings' on it."

I put it on and wore it all night. But I have not seen anything on it yet. I think it will show up things now and then.

October 28 or 29

In the Alone Room, I asked Jesus, "When--how soon is soon with my teeth?"

Jesus said, "The day that you have your birthday is the day that you and your Mom, and Mama will have it!"

"Angels told me yesterday that it would be very soon. The tickle angels were all over me, and one was brushing my teeth. It was sort of a vision."

It had been several years of believing her very bad teeth would be healed. It was her choice to 'get new teeth,' instead of trying to fix them. It ensued a faith journey of her own. Other than no pain, we had not seen evidence of healing, or new teeth until Xrays showed new teeth underneath looking good.

> *"I was in the Love Room. I would call it the Presence Room because His Love flows out of His Presence."*

NOVEMBER 22

Thanksgiving at Aunt June's. Rachel talked about past fears, since she was small—beings and voices in the walls of her room, evil woman outside. How she always wanted her door shut to keep them out, wanted somebody to sleep with her, etc. I had always wondered why she didn't want her door open—to feel closer to us just down the hall?

"After the 'fixing waterfall' (which happened in the Philippines) went into my brain, and fixed part of it, I was filled with God's Love, and all the fear was gone! The angels were singing, 'Oh how I love you! Oh how He loves me. .'"

I needed that years and years ago! I don't know why it didn't happen before. I felt Him near me a lot since then. He whispered that He loved me.

Angels usually sing loud. I asked how the angels could heal. They get it from God, and bring it to us the same way we get it and take it to others.

DECEMBER

I was wandering around Heaven by myself again. I discovered a room that even the angels or some people didn't know about. A little music was playing. This room was meant for people on earth to use and for people to 'get saved.' In Heaven they say, 'Getting their hearts healed'.

I twisted a thing that looked like a jack-in-the-box with the turner on top. It made wonderful music and people were getting their hearts healed.

When I went out, Jesus and the angels were celebrating all around me.

> *As I am editing this journal for printing—at the turn of the year into 2014— this part about wandering around Heaven really struck me. I knew it was meant for us this year. What a wonderful picture of us in our daily life! Wandering around Heaven, hearing some nice soft music; healing starts happening while we are playing at our work station—the work that used to be the daily grind— round and round—now is a music box that heals people's hearts, while I am wandering around Heaven, and hearing the music, and playing, and getting healed, other people are getting healed too!*
>
> *And, then I become aware that Jesus and the angels are celebrating all around me. I am in awe, wondering how long they have been doing this! And, then I remember they have been doing this since before Time began. As I barely dare to breathe for fear of 'waking up', I hear Him say, "Just stay. You can live here if you want." And, I can see in His eyes, He really, really wants me to. Then I say, "It's what I have always wanted."*
>
> *You can join me if you want to, with expectations mounting up on wings of eagles—soaring to heights unknown..exploring..resting..wandering around as if we are Free! While people around us wonder why we are so 'lit up' at our work station—why we can't stop smiling..or singing..or loving..why everything we touch turns to gold. And then, I came across another excerpt that has to go with this:*

. . Knowing His Love is like play-work in Heaven. On earth is different. It happens while I'm working; I hear His Love through my heart ears. Most is Jesus' part. Mine part is only to believe. His part is to tell me and show me.

> *Back to Jesus and angels singing—*

All the people started coming out of other rooms and places, to join in. Somebody I sort of recognized came too*

The celebration was for 'healed hearts'—dancing like at a Ball, but with food and wine. (God's wine and bread is not like earth stuff.) When Jesus turned water to wine, it was Heaven Wine. The people drank only a little and fell to the floor, laughing and laughing, like stuck to the floor!!!

*My dad's parents, who I had seen on earth, asking where their son was—now were in Heaven.

This was Granny and Papa who had gone to Heaven before Rachel was born. So she is referring to the previous dream when they had 'stopped in'!

They said to me, "Next time, bring your dad to Heaven."

It seemed so real. I thought Dad was sleeping in the room. So I didn't want to answer, in case I would wake him.

"How do you know who I am? Last time it seemed like you didn't even recognize me."

"At first we didn't know you. We thought you were just a little girl from the street, or orphan or something. But now we know our grandchildren." They brought me in. This was the first time I talked to my family in Heaven. Other times when I saw them, they didn't talk to me.

Most people in Heaven do work with children. I asked, "Where's Heather and Tami's babies?"

They said, "Babies that are not born yet are not in the nursery. It's a separate place for those who are going to earth."

"I want to see them!" I said.

The angel said, "You'll have to wait a night (of earth zone time). And, the second time will be on earth very soon."

December 7

In Heaven, I saw a couple familiar people. "How do I recognize you, if I don't know you?"

"We met a few years ago. . " they said.

"But I was just passing through the room. I just saw your eyes." I said. They grew up in Heaven. And their angels come down to comfort their mothers. Also, loved ones come down and stay weeks or months at a time.

It seemed like everyone in Heaven is married to the Lord.

They asked me, "Why are you here?"

"To show you the Memory Room, your best memories, and some you don't even know about." It was like I was always there, but didn't know it. Angels don't even know about all the rooms in Heaven!

The mystery of Heaven is you don't normally know everything. What you think and say is not what it is. The angels said, "If you would have believed, you would have seen all the rooms of Heaven by now."

"The Throne looked different when I was little," I said. "Thank you for showing me."

They said, "People won't get it. .when they talk about gold." Children know when I talk about it, even if they haven't experienced. Gold means something about FREEDOM. It's not a color, or money. So, they believe you (in Heaven) when you say, 'America has gold!' FREEDOM! FREEDOM! FREEDOM!

On earth adults think you're rich. But the children know it's freedom. I've said it to other countries too. Angel language works good because you can plan surprises. You can say it out loud, because most people don't understand—even people in Heaven.

Babies know and do everything in Heaven. They don't have to learn and practice like on earth. Angels take care of them until they are big enough for mothers or grandmothers to care for. Other people don't visit or know about the babies, unless Jesus or the angels show them that room.

These were some wonderful things of Heaven that we talked about.

> "Gold means something about FREEDOM. It's not a color, or money."

December 22

I was in Heaven with many angels in The Meeting Room area—a place where people go to meet angels. I met my Surprise Angel—who isn't only mine. She has lots of other people.

She doesn't tell me lots of stuff. She just says, "Come to The Meeting Room." She always keeps things a surprise.

So I said to her, "Am I staying in here the whole entire night ?" (That was the first time I used the word 'night'—the earth zone word).

She said, "No, but you will come back here at the end." She knows lots of people's languages. She is hundreds of people's angel, in many countries. She doesn't speak ALL languages, but lots.

Next to The Future Room was another room. It was new. She didn't know the name of it. None of the angels know. It's a hidden name. Wonderful things from God flowing all together throughout and to earth. Angels didn't name this room. When Jesus names it, they don't know.

The Surprise Angel 'gets it' when you tell her stuff. She looks all different ways at different times to different people—maybe dark pink, or gold, or other. Most angels always look the same.

This 'Mystery Room' is connected to The Alone Room, and The Future Room. It's all mixed up together with earth, and in us, and GOD, in Heaven, and connected to our bodies. *(This came with a lot of hand motions!)*

It gets bigger as more things are attached!

At this point, Rachel and I noticed the fourth rainbow that appeared on my bed, from the sun coming through the prism in my window. Numerous little rainbows appeared on us, and around the room, morning after morning during these precious times of Heaven touching earth. The privilege of seeing and feeling God and our real Home, brought to me—to us all—by a child! Connecting, transforming, life-ing, enlightening us—in Presence, in Spirit and in Truth.

When I went back to the meeting place, I met the Promise Angel. She makes plans with people and helps Surprise Angel. They work together. As they do their jobs, it helps each other at the same time as it helps people.

When angels work together, they are 'sisters' and can look like one big angel. So that's why sometimes they have two different names, but look like one big angel. That might be mostly for kids' first time visits, to be less confusing.

The kids see this room as a living room. They see more as they visit more often.

DECEMBER 26

I was in Heaven in a different room. Lots of people had wings, including me! "But, why do I have smaller wings than anybody?" Mostly wings are the same size.

"You are just starting to experience..in each room is the beginning of a new experience. So the more you discover this room, the bigger your wings get. This room isn't only for celebration. It is also called The Praying Hospital."

People walk through and the Spirit is praying through them—not them praying. You walk through for yourself to be healed, or for people all over the world. In one or two nights, it can spread all over the world.

You can come anytime. Sometimes only Jesus is there praying. I knew He did that in the Bible, but I didn't know He would do that in Heaven!

The angel said, "He is your soul. He is praying inside of you. But you can see Him out of you."

It's inside of you—the angels and Jesus. When you go to Heaven, you go inside your soul. Sounds weird, but other people have experienced this. It sounds cool. . amazing! Heaven is a little circle I walk through.

At first it looks like a BIG MOUNTAIN—Heaven in your soul! And I always had a question—'How do I see it that way?' It was just a 'click' and I'm there! So, how do I take other people? All different ways:

Tell them about Heaven and they will eventually go.

Sometimes I say 'FREEDOM' and 'GOLD' which means freedom to go to Heaven at the same time grabbing their arm.

Different things work for different people.

Tell them to dream of Heaven.

For people who don't know Jesus:
First step—Tell them about Him with them experiencing Him.
Second—Tell about Heaven.
Third—Believe and you go there.

I don't know how I started to go there. But, you can help people by telling them to dream. Also tell their bodies to remember, even if they are 'nothing dreams'. I tell my brother and sister, but they have to believe they can. Lots of people think you're crazy. But it does help. . to tell people. You help them through this third step.

Many people, in a Heaven visit, believe and are changed. When they wake up, they might not even know, or think it's weird that it actually happened.

Going to Heaven is a BIG PRESENT! Many children would know, because they have gone there. I haven't met them here, but some I have met in Heaven. Laughing dreams.

If you ask them "How much LOVE does God have?"

They would say, "He is so deep, and so high—like a mountain! He is so loving, you can't count it! You can't understand it!"

> "You walk through for yourself to be healed, or for people all over the world. In one or two nights, it can spread through all over the world."

ANOTHER DREAM

It was a visit to some lady's house. She prayed heart prayers, and lives forever still. . maybe in a Muslim country.

She knew how to count the stars. That goes with knowing the Love. It's amazing! The stars don't re-sent (represent) how BIG He is. They re-sent how much Love He has.

(Mama) "Now, we can go out under the stars and let His Love twinkle and shine and shower on us, and soak into us LOVE. . boundless, unending !" The sun and the stars are always shining on us—always.

I talked to another woman about Heaven and she didn't say anything. She could talk and talk and talk with people who believed like her. Finally, I said, "What are you saying?"

Her sister had come to believe. And she prayed every a.m. and p.m. "Help me to know more LOVE of You," which is what many people pray in their hearts.

You WILL know how much He loves <u>before</u> He comes back!

Many people don't listen. They just pray their words, close their eyes and see nothing. They don't let Him answer the prayer of their hearts. (Simply profound! Profoundly simple!)

I wait with my eyes closed and know more and more and more of His love. Or get a picture.

So, what are we waiting for?

Joy rain

43

January 2013
Age Ten

JANUARY 4

I went to find Promise and Surprise. I got there—to the Angel Meeting Room. We went out—where were they taking me? I had not seen this before, even though it was always there.

I was going up Heaven's stairs, 'Heaven walking'—like flying, floating. I went past my room. (Every woman has a room where they keep special things, and stay to rest sometimes.)

We came to The Baby Angel Meeting Room. They all invited me to their own special rooms which are hard to find. Normally, it only happens by accident. They like to hide them (smile). I had to pass through the Ball Room, also called The Jewel Room. There was a 'stage' where Jesus stands. But it's not called a stage in Heaven.

When I got to their room, an angel was there helping them. She looked weird, in a crazy, crazy dress, with a colorful apron that had a big bunch on the side. And she was a cook.

"How does she cook?" It's hard to describe. She puts things on the children—like if they got burned, she makes it like they never got burned. One of her many nicknames is Fire Angel, like in the Bible, the fiery furnace.

To the baby angels, she is Mother. She does 'cook'. It's fast and easy to cook in Heaven. She just passes through the room, and the tea is there. You don't usually see her, though sometimes she sits and eats too.

The room is almost as pretty as the Jewel Room. Because when a room is close to another and you go through it to get there, it is very similar.

JANUARY 8

In Heaven again! Whatever I saw was BEAUTIFUL! I don't know what it was. And people that have been there a thousand years don't know either. Many just stay in the room where all the people are—that kinda looks like earth. They don't much go to other rooms like The Alone Room with Jesus.

This is the Dancing Room. It's HUGE! I see people who have lost somebody on earth (before they died and came here).

They say some people don't die before they go there. Their heart is in Heaven, but they're still living on earth. The saying is God takes you to Heaven, before you're ready. It sounds confusing. But, you can get it, if you know what it means. They are living on earth and Heaven at the same time. Their spirit is taken to Heaven. I know people in Heaven that live on earth, but I don't know them down here.

It doesn't make sense, but sometimes people are there that don't know Jesus. I've seen a little girl, and I asked her 100 times, "Do you know Jesus?" They know about Him, but not in their heart. They are there to learn to know Him in their hearts.

Many people on earth don't know God loves them. At night they can go to Heaven to experience His Love. That's why I first went to Heaven.

Some people God is taking their spirit to Heaven, but they just 'let go'.

I used to do that, 'cause I didn't know. You have to hold on. You have to believe.

Letting go is: believing more in Hell—scared in the spirit. You get grabbed away.

Holding on is: 'I want to know Your Love'—in your spirit—even if it's not in your mind. Many people don't know about their spirit, so they don't know it's happening. Hundreds in Heaven, and on earth, are believers in their spirit, but not in their mind.

Sometimes your mind can disconnect in a good way. Or, accidently, by the devil. Then it pumps down, instead of like it is supposed to pump up.

That's what happened to me (in the Philippines) when He changed my mind. God heals people's minds, but they don't know it at first. Then they keep saying the same things as before. In a way, my mind was always healed, but I didn't know it until I had the wonderful experience.

Before, I believed Hell was real, and Heaven was not, so my mind 'pumped down'. Don't let your mind get caught, meaning pump 'down'. People get healed when they let their spirit 'pump up'.

You can give your heart to God. But they can easily grab onto Satan. Many in Heaven have given their hearts to God, but not what's connected to it—their mind. So they are easily grabbed partly onto Satan. It can go either way.

Lies come the most when you're not feeling the best. Satan is trying to get me disconnected. A tower of gates gets built in the mind when you keep believing lies. It grows to the top of your head and blocks the spirit.

It can open for a minute, but close again with believing lies. Make sure Who is catching your eye!

It happens in marriage too. It might seem like a man and woman don't go together. But any man and woman can go together. They can love each other. They won't let Satan control their marriage.

Getting divorced doesn't mean you don't love each other. You just let Satan control. If God controls your marriage, no one would get divorced. It doesn't matter which person. . it's just who controls the marriage.

Many people experience this all the time—partly God and partly Satan—and they can't tell the difference. I am learning. I can tell when it's Satan; it's like make-believe. He's not really alive. He's dead in Hell. It doesn't say that in the Bible. But God took me to Hell to see that Satan and his men are dead. He's just a statue.

> *"Many people don't listen. They just pray their words, close their eyes and see nothing. They don't let Him answer the prayer of their hearts."*

January 12

I saw a beautiful something??? and I asked, "What does it mean, or re-(pre)sent?"

'Angel Teller', Laurie, is an angel who answers lots of questions. She said, "It's not an earth waterfall, but a sort of Heaven waterfall—though I don't know exactly. But, I've been told it normally means. . glory, promises, all different stuff.

After that, I went to the place I've been going a lot—The Secret Place.

It's where people usually end up when they visit. It's like coming in the back—not walls and gates, but outside like a garden, and quiet.

I asked Jesus, "What do you want to do? Or what do you want to ask me, or show me?" ('Cuz I didn't have any questions like what should I write, or encourage.)

He just took my hand, and we went past the hole where people come up through to Heaven. We looked down on earth. It looked like diamonds, diamond-shaped! "Why?"

He said, "The people are like diamonds to me! How beautiful you are! I look to the heart. I look to the spirit. And, they are beautiful!

I asked, "Is that scripture?"

He answered, "Yes, but in different words." It was His own translation.

I said, "I'm going down there."

He said, "You need to."

I felt I would like to tell them how beautiful they were, and encourage them. Jesus doesn't use people the way you would think. He normally uses me to go down (like an angel), to encourage. Some people are more for healing or miracles. But I am good at encouraging people, and with my dreams. People don't always know what they're meant to do. Jesus told me a long time ago about sharing my dreams. Now I know how to encourage. I know what to say.

As I went down, the diamonds were getting bigger. They were lighted

I was getting closer. "What am I supposed to do here?"

"Go over here."

In three steps, there was a woman. "Why are you crying?"

"I don't have any talent. I've done everything, and tried other peoples', and I just can't."

"Well, have you tried encouraging people?"

"No."

"Well, let's go!"

"Where?"

It looked like a mountain, where you go up. But, it's quick. As we went up she stopped crying. She said, "Where are we going? And, how will we get there?"

"To Heaven. It's not far. It's here."

She looked back down and said, "earth looks so beautiful! Like diamonds!" She kept looking down 'til we got there, (about five minutes earth time). It was her first time in Heaven. "It's so beautiful! Where is the rest of it?"

"There's lots of parts. But because of the way I took you up, you can see the most beautiful-est, beautiful-est parts!" It's the only words I could think of to use. She was seeing down to earth diamonds!

Jesus grabbed her hand after she had been in the hole for a while, to prepare. He said, "I want to show you the beauty of Heaven, and tell you secrets and stuff."

They talked about her talents. And He asked if she was ready to encourage people. She just kept answering, "Yes! Yes! Yes!"

He had her slide down the water slide. She asked how to encourage people. He gave her a book, which she didn't understand. So He explained how the heart mailboxes work—dropping pages into their spirits.

She said she could believe that. "So where's my pen?"

Jesus laughed, "Right there!" pointing to her mouth! "When you close your eyes (on the earth), you will see yourself with Me, writing in the book."

Then she realized when she was crying, with her eyes closed, that it was a vision. As soon as she got back down, she realized that I hadn't actually grabbed her body, and took her to Heaven.

Now she was crying happy cries, and saw herself running through the streets with two letters in her hands. Then they slipped back through her heart to Heaven.

She was so happy about this vision, she drove all the way to her mother's house. Her mother said, "Are you sure it was a vision?"

"Yes!"

Her mother said, "I know who you planted a seed in." It was in her brother's heart!

> "He said, "The people are like diamonds to me! How beautiful you are!
> I look to the heart. I look to the spirit. And, they are beautiful!"

JANUARY 14

I was in Heaven. I went the spirit way, by myself. I didn't take anyone with me. I said to Jesus, "What are you doing today, or-r-r what am I doing?" I didn't have to go through the preparing place.

He showed me the most beautiful part of the place—the Secret Place where I always have been going. It was a waterfall that sparkled like diamonds (the Rock that you slide down looks like a slide, and with a landing. But, that's a different waterfall).

Lots of rooms have something that controls how pretty they are. This waterfall controls how pretty this place is. Jesus took me down it, and it didn't stop. It kept going and going and going 'til it got down to earth.

"Why doesn't it stop?"

"The others are for encouragement. This one is just for fun!—to go down to earth. It has the same power—miracle water. Jesus calls it Heaven water. It heals, and if people have been sad their whole life, when they drink, they are happy again.

Mama starts singing: DRINKING AT THE SPRINGS OF LIVING WATER. HAPPY NOW AM I! MY SOUL IS SATISFIED!. .

"Why am I brought down here with You?"

Jesus didn't think that was a stupid question. He said, "Because people want to meet you."

"Isn't it my time to stay down here?"

"No, we are going the heart mailbox way."

"I thought I already did."

"No, we are going up the waterfall, also called, the Letter Waterfall."

He showed me different ways to send letters, or to go up and down with Him. He showed me different kinds of tools. These tools aren't for building, but for healing peoples' hearts. It starts to be built before they decide they want to know Jesus. In their minds it's building blocks that block the right things. It's easy, and doesn't take a long time.

Jesus said, "Right after you were born, it started to get built. In the Heaven realm, you would look grown up. The reason you see yourself as a kid is 'cuz you're always with Me. And I see you as a kid."

When grown-ups come to Heaven, they are surprised because they see themselves as nine or ten, or maybe thirteen. When they get to know Jesus, the angels see them as grown up. Their walls have been built. But, they can be broken. If there is something in your mind, it can end up in your heart, because the walls are broken. But it can easily be built back.

If they believed they were sick for a long time, that part of the wall is partly broke down years ago. Then, they can get sick again. But, when you say, 'I'm healed! I'm healed!'—then it gets built pretty quickly.

A testimony of a girl—her building totally broke. If your body controls your heart, then you can keep getting sick. Things that happen then can control your heart. It isn't the devil. It's what you believe.

Bad thoughts normally happen, not because of believing wrong. It's because of what you watch, or what you hear in the streets, or thoughts that just go through your mind. The devil doesn't have power to tell lies. For example. . with food, you think it's bad because of what you've heard about it—how people have ruined it. It matters how you believe. If you really think it will make you sick, it will.

A saying in Heaven—'You got your shirt dirty'—really means your building is dirty from wrong believing. And after a while it will start breaking down (this isn't about your body, but about your spirit).

The song I woke up with—He was singing into my heart, but I didn't know 'til I woke up.

> *I love you, Little Daughter.*
> *You're so beautiful to Me.*
> *You're one of my favorite people.*
> *You are all my favorite people.*
> *The Father is my Temple, my hiding place.*
> *The Holy Spirit in Me, in you, is my Father.*
> *All the birds in Heavenly places make beautiful songs.*
> *Singing about you!*
> *How beautiful you are! How wonderful you are!*
> *How amazing you are! How wonderful you are!*
> *How wonderful you are!*

The first night He was showing me how much He loved me. The second, He was telling me.

It ended with this song.

JANUARY 15

In the past my building got dirty. Then it broke. But, He didn't talk about the past. He said, "When you finally decided to give your heart to me," (when I was little) "your building started. And, you were letting it build during the night. And, during the day, it was breaking down." My heart was more attached to His Love during the night.

Jesus said, "As you let it grow, listening to Me in your natural mind, it's like a seed. If you don't listen, the seed will start to die, which is the same as the building breaking." When He reminds me of whatever He told me, it's like a new seed gets planted. My favorite story in the Bible is about the seeds.

The rest of the dream was just about Him pouring out His Love on Me. *(Lots of hand motions).* It was so wonderful! I had always wanted to go on the slide alone with Him. And I always wanted to see the pretty parts of that place.

I remember smiling at Him and laughing. These two dreams are the best I've had because I felt how much He loves me. He grabbed onto my shoulders and told me His Love. And, He said the more you know His Love, the more the work gets built in Heaven. It's not what you do, as most people think. That's just not true at all.

People just think in earth zone. But, I can't say that to them (chuckle).

The more I know His Love, the more my plant is growing, or, the building is getting built. Knowing His Love is like play-work in Heaven. In earth is different. It happens while I'm working; I hear His Love through my heart ears. Most is Jesus' part. My part is only to believe. His part is to tell me and show me.

JANUARY 17

I was in Heaven, and saw angels doing a play. "I thought you only do a play on Christmas Eve?"

They said, "We call it Festival Eve. And we sometimes do it just for the children, because they like watching. Other times we do it to celebrate Jesus. We do it just for Him."

"And, what do you do the next day?" (Smile) How can it be the next day? I guess it's like when you take a nap, then it's the next day. . a nap in His Grace.

They celebrate in different ways all the time. It's in different places, so I haven't experienced them. The festivals are different than feasts, where you have food. You may have drinks, but you're never hungry in Heaven. When you get drunk either by Heaven wine, or by this glory drink, you get more of His Love. When I got drunk for the first time in the Philippines, I was drinking the glory drink.

Celebrating in different ways—you don't always know what. Sometimes they celebrate for kids, and before a baby gets in someone's tummy.

When I was typing this—from what had been written in the journal—I suddenly stopped typing to declare with conviction in my spirit, NO MORE DELAY! for Heather and Tami! ALREADY OVER-DUE to be pregnant! Then I turned the page, to finish typing and what I had forgotten followed, from 2 month ago!

"And, He said the more you know His Love, the more the work gets built in Heaven. It's not what you do, as most people think. That's just not true at all."

Then I asked, "What about Heather and Tami?"

They said, "You don't always know how soon is 'real soon'". . (which they had told me before).

"Will I get to see them now?"

The angel said, "Come with me." The babies were meant to come earlier. I don't know why they are late. They were in a different room than all the other babies who are ready to go. So they have grown a little Like—it should have been a couple years ago.

"Because of their bodies, they can't have babies?"

"No. The reason is the babies don't want to go down there—to have mothers."

"Why?"

"Some do and some don't. It takes some a long time to decide. because they like Heaven so much. We don't say, 'No' to babies, because in Heaven nothing is wrong."

It is hard to explain. Unless you're asking a question about something you can't understand, or see—then they will answer 'yes' or, 'no' or, 'some day soon.' But, if the babies go down, they could come back to visit, or they could just spend their whole life just on earth. It makes a lot of difference what they believe. There's a lot of confusion on earth.

I asked, "Why can't you just take them down? Then, their tummies will be bigger right away. If they don't want to come, why don't you tell them they'll be back again someday?"

"Because they will think 'soon' is just a couple of years. Even though they're born and can't talk, in Heaven they talk and understand. Then on earth they forget what they knew in Heaven." They forget more than children, or grown-ups do.

I knew what Tami's and Heather's babies looked like. Heather will maybe have twins, but sometimes it gets changed—because one is better. It sounds like the doctor is wrong. But, really, its because it got changed in Heaven. I heard that about Heather.

Actually, my daughter, Heather, is a twin. Her sister, Holly, has four children. And, they have often wondered if either of them would have twins. So, this was especially interesting to us.

I only saw one for each. But there is another that isn't born out of the angel's tummy yet (That's how they first come. Then she is your special angel all your life. When I first met Laughy, I knew her. And, she was the only angel who spoke my language.) It is the angels, not Jesus, who decide when they go down.

"What are their names going to be?"

"We don't exactly know, but Jesus' advice was, 'Flower' and 'Diamond'," which were my imaginary friends! I was so surprised! But, that's how He sees them.

Rachel says there are lots of nicknames in Heaven. When Heather heard, she said, "I have had the name, Lily, picked for a long time!"

The angel said, "The babies are starting to say, 'I'm going to be ready to go really soon."

"But, how soon is really soon?"

"If they say, 'I'm ready,' then, it is NOW. But it depends on their decision. They might always say, 'I'm not ready.' But if they say, 'really soon', then it takes at least 3 days, and 3 hours, or at most, 3 years.

I asked the angel, "Why can't you decide that they could see Heaven the whole entire time?"

"It partly depends on what they believe—what they want," the angel said. And, when they want to, there might be a waiting until the angel gets things ready. (This was part of a discussion with Mama who is always asking to visit and stay in Heaven!)

Angels have so many jobs, it seems. Like example, busy with bringing babies back to Heaven from mommies' tummies. Then, when they get a little bigger, grandmothers take care of them.

Rachel is talking about aborted babies, and grandmothers who are living in Heaven.

Another reason angels are busy—they have to go down all the time because people are worried.

"Why don't you have them come up here?"

"Because the people don't grab our hand." They just look at everything around, and don't grab on to the angel above them. They have to think about Jesus, and good things, or they won't see. They won't grab on. They have to look up—where the angels are coming.

My angels were always coming when I was little, but, I always looked 'to the edge.' I was having two dreams at the same time. I have to look away from the bad, and think different. I have to say different than what I'm seeing. This happens a lot. My mind is still a little confused because I'm seeing both.

People in Heaven (visiting Heaven) saw angels all around their room, but they grabbed onto the right set. I've experienced that. It looks make-believe, like toys. You have to choose. It's like a computer game, with arrows. I never choose any of it. . because it's wrong! Wrong! Wrong! Wrong! WRONG!

Then, this funny guy puts light on when he comes into the room—paper, plastic, like a projector. It's not good. When I tell him to go, I have to tell him to take his papers with him. Whatever you see in the room can control things. So what do you see? In dreams?

The children say, "I see goodness all around."

Grown-ups say, "There's no goodness here; no goodness in the earth."

Sometimes I go down to real earth, not just in the spirit.

At the end of the dream, I heard the babies say, "I think we'll be ready in 3 days." That's what the angels had told me.

"Will they get to see Heaven again soon?"

They didn't say 'no', so it is maybe 'yes.' The angels I was talking to were not angels I knew. Some of them were angel mothers.

Tami & Heather have been married for 10 years, waiting for children. So, considering this dream, and the first mention in December, concerning timing—'real soon', and, '3+ days' to '3 years', we were very encouraged! We have learned, with Rachel's time, that a Heaven day is a month on earth.

Note that Rachel got to see the babies a month later (a Heaven day). As the angel had said, "You'll have to wait a night (of earth zone time). And, the second time will be on earth very soon."

Can you imagine our excitement, when 3+ months later Heather called with a big announcement?!! Heather—who is younger—was mentioned first, possibly significant. Now, we await a call from Tami!

JANUARY 25

I was in Heaven, and I saw a beautiful Heaven rainbow waterfall in Heaven colors. It started way up high, and came down on my head. Every time it landed, it landed on someone's head. And they felt His Love and Promises that He made in Heavenly places, not on earth.

Then I walked right up to Him. "What do you want me to do here?"

"Come with Me." He took me to a place that looked like a pool. But He said it wasn't. He showed me a switch. When I turned it on, hundreds of waterfalls came down! Jesus likes to surprise you with things that you think you know, but they're totally different. It was like a kiddie pool but it was a 'Waterfall Keeper'. It stored the waterfalls that come into your spirit, so it would never run out.

"Why are you showing me?"

"Because I love you, daughter. These are the rivers of Love, and some of Joy. Also another river, the River of Youth—if you let it flow.

"How do I do it?"

"Just by believing. And, say it's already happening," when it's not. because it helps somehow.

"Is this all You are showing me tonight?"

"I'm not going to tell you, because it's a surprise." Then He took me to the horse stables, and said, "Just get on the horse with Me. You can ride your horse later."

So I got on with Him. I had waited years to ride with Him! (But, years on the earth are like minutes in Heaven. You can go back in time in Heaven. But if you see future it's like a picture in the Future Room. Time is very different there.)

The horse started running—like random, like it didn't have to go a certain way. With two people on, the horse goes fast so they can stay on. Usually horses walk in Heaven, and we don't tell them how fast to go. So, this was a little scary, though nothing is really scary in Heaven. Jesus said it can go much faster yet. If there were ten people on, it would go really, really fast!

When we finally got there, I didn't see anything. "You led me to nowhere!" I said.

Jesus just laughed.

Then I saw a table, and angels, and a room. They had cakes—not with sugar. They are good for your spirit. They have joy and peace. They were lighting the candles on it, and singing, 'Happy Birthday!'

"But, it's not my birthday! It's months away." But in Heaven, they celebrate anytime. It's outside 'Time', remember? So it was a surprise party.

Jesus said, "Open your gifts first!"

I opened a flute, and Jesus said to blow it. It played the Love song that Jesus sang when I first came to Heaven. It's the one He sings to everyone when they first come. He said, "There will be more songs, but this is the only one you know now."

The next gift was a box to keep musical instruments in. So I put the flute in it.

Jesus said, "There is another gift here, from Laughy."

She wasn't there because she was exploring Heaven with someone else. Angles can only be in one place at a time. And if they have to be someplace on earth or something, they can't just go someplace else. Only Jesus can be in more places at the same time

The present was very beautifully wrapped—a color we don't have on earth. When I opened it, it was a picture with the name and a little bit about each of my angels.

I said, "Can you tell Laughy 'thank you' when you see her?"

Part of it could spin. Everytime I turned it, it was a different song. It was an angel song box—not like a music box on earth. But, like you could see the angel pictures actually singing, making the music.

I put it in the Instrument Box. And, when the angels told Laughy how much I liked the gift, she said, "I knew she would."

Jesus said, "I can't explain anymore to you, because you wouldn't understand." He said this about the last gift He gave me—which wasn't one you could unwrap.

He said, "I can only explain it in Heaven language, and you don't understand enough words. You will see it during the day with your eyes open."

"But, how will I know?"

So, when I woke up, Jesus was standing there. Then I knew. He said, "I love you, Daughter."

Then I was sort of in a daydream, with my eyes open. "I love you, Jesus."

Then, He took me back up to Heaven. There was a diamond. And He said, "Stand on top of it."

That seemed impossible, but I did it. I was in different colors. My normal clothes turned into a beautiful dress—a jean dress.

He said, "Put your hand on the sleeve." When I did, it made music! I started singing with it. Then Heaven fireworks started—not loud like earth, but with music sounds.

He said, "Touch the fireworks."

I was concerned about getting burned. Plus it seemed impossible to touch things way up in the sky. But I did it. And I felt like I was burning up. He told me Heaven fire is like drops of water. In three minutes, I started feeling wet, then turned to ice—ice drops on me.

"Squeeze them," He said.

When I squeezed them, three diamonds came out:

1—Freedom,
2—Love (love song),
3—Joy (laughing while you sing).

I put those in my box too. This was the most wonderful place I have been.

Jesus said, "It's a Diamond Heaven Dress-up Place!"

JANUARY 29

I was in Heaven with Jesus. And I said to Him, "What do you want me to do?"

"Nothing really. All I want is for you to know my love, to experience it. And though it is partly my job, it's also yours—to believe what you have been told."

Then I dropped something that was in my hand. It wasn't really sin but it was getting too heavy. Jesus said, "Just drop it on the ground, or the earth." When it hits the earth, it's a big bag of sand!

Jesus said, "I carried all of it for you—all the sin. I tied it all on Me- to the cross. I didn't carry my sin; I carried your sin. You were with my disciples there, standing with Me."

"Why was it that one of your disciples gave You to your enemies?"

"It wouldn't have worked any other way. God had it planned that way. I had to do this."

People saw Jesus go up, but He also went down to a low part of Heaven. He didn't just keep going up, up, up.

"Why did you make people think You were just going up?"

"I had to go up to see my Father. But then I came back to the lower parts to be with my people. I need to be where they can find Me. Lots of things happen on earth for purpose, for good purpose. I'm showing you in another way how much I love you."

So I was down on my knees again, crying and seeing His knees with the blood. "I love you so-o-o much, Jesus. Thank You. I love you. ."

He showed me the Father dressed like a King. And Jesus was dressed as a Shepherd. I never saw them different like that. But they trade places sometimes. They are both the King.

The Father said to me, "You know I love you as much as My Son loves you. Come with Me."

He showed me the most beautiful room in Heaven. Even though all the rooms in Heaven are beautiful, this was more.

Then the Holy Spirit popped out of my spirit. He was all gold, a golden man. Remember—gold means FREEDOM. This is to keep your mind free of thinking wrong, and your spirit free to see what Heaven is like. I went into the Holy Spirit. His outside was Protector.

> *"All I want is for you to know my love, to experience it. And though it is partly my job, it's also yours—to believe what you have been told."*

"People on earth call Him Holy Spirit" Father said, "I called Him JOY. Jesus added—AND. So He's JOYAND in Heaven."

"That is different. What does that mean?"

"It means Joy Whisper. When Jesus died Holy Spirit was in Him, so He died as well. Then they came back to life. And you were with Him in the tomb."

Jesus had told me a long time ago, "When you finally see the Holy Spirit in Heaven, the Father will be dressed like a King, and I will be a Shepherd." And this was the time!

I was crying—for His Love, and saying, "Thank you! Thank You!" I never had thought about the Father taking me anywhere. It was all a surprise.

Father said, "I didn't plan this; Jesus did."

When I walked back to Jesus, still crying in happy cries, He told me from now on the Father will be walking with me! It seemed like a weird (meaning 'amazing, unreal') dream—even for Heaven. But it was always my dream. I just didn't know it could happen!

People said, "You are so lucky. It is impossible. . "They even say that in Heaven. But, impossible is only on the earth. And, now, when I am walking on the earth, nothing seems impossible to me—no matter if I'm in Heaven, or on earth. If it's possible in Heaven, it is possible on earth. If things are that way in Heaven, they can be that way on earth.

When people see impossibilities, I just say, "It's already happened." Like miracles, dreams, seeing the Father—not like sticky in my hair or something—but things that come true every day, things that GOD does. If you let GOD guide you through, nothing is impossible.

Why can't we get ourselves well? So many of us try to do stuff ourselves, instead of just letting GOD do it. Even if you take medicine, say, "GOD is the one who makes me well."

Sometimes if you take stuff, and you don't have faith in GOD getting you well, you might get worse. You can take it, or not take it, the point is what you believe. Do you trust GOD?

I had just heard from a prophetic friend regarding the flu, "Do what you need to do, but don't trust in what you do." This part of Rachel's dream revelations was directly answering my night conversations/questions with the Lord.

You might say, "Why am I still sick?" Part of your body still sees yourself sick. Sometimes, a part—not my brain—but a hand or something tells me I am. We're still learning, and we don't have to do anything about it. GOD will just heal it.

He sees us all healed. But, He says it matters what you think, what you see.

Part of everyone's mind has the wrong thinking. It's been put in through the years. He says, "Your physical body has some wrong thinking in it."

Some people have all their lives had right thinking, and they don't get sick. Bad things happen in the world because of wrong belief systems *(not usually in Rachel's vocabulary)*. If everybody believes right, then all fear, all bad things would be GONE!

Rachel raised her voice, which she seldom does during these accounts, and dramatically made the sign an umpire does for SAFE!

Everyone's big WHY is, 'Why are there bad things in the earth?'

Jesus gave me this answer, because I asked. "Just because of what you (people) believed over the years. I see you perfect. But, it's how do you see?"

We have to believe our whole entire mind is healed, and no wrong thinking. When wrong thoughts accidently come in—I don't want to use the word 'try' to think right—I just don't hang on to them.

You asked how to completely believe when you have earth facts problems.

One—Don't even think of hanging on to the wrong thinking!

And, two—Say it's healed!

"And, now, when I am walking on the earth, nothing seems impossible to me—no matter if I'm in heaven, or on earth. If it's possible in heaven, it is possible on earth. If things are that way in heaven, they can be that way on earth."

February 2013
Age Ten

FEBRUARY 1

I was in Heaven, and I saw Jesus. He took me to His place. I can't really explain it. "This is so beautiful! Why did You show me this?!"

"Because I wanted to show you my Love in this beautiful part of Heaven."

Then we went to the third Alone Room. I encouraged three people with the pages of paper.

Then Jesus took me down to His bedroom. He sat down on the bed. Then I sat down as He got up. I felt His Love coming up from my soul, my heart, and jumped up to my brain. I was crying at His knees. .

Then I ran down a hill. That's what you do when you're so happy. And, I said, "I love You so much!"

And, He was saying it from His heart—showing me instead of talking. "I love you, my Daughter."

FEBRUARY 7

I was in Heaven. Jesus said, "Come with Me."

Where we went, I had been before. Now I really needed it (on the earth). It doesn't have a name written on it. Jesus said, "It's the Room of Spirit." This is different than Holy Spirit. Only certain people know what it is called.

I can describe it better now, because I saw more of it. This room shows what is happening—good things when you're just in your body, like, out of your spirit. I really needed to be there because I wasn't having a very good day. I was missing what God was trying to show because my body just didn't let me.

As I looked, it was like my little house, just a kitchen and a bedroom. "Why a kitchen in Heaven?—when we don't need to cook?"

He said, "Just open the oven."

I did, and in it was the word LOVE. In the microwave was the word JOY. And, under the sink where water comes was PEACE. Those are the main ingredients that every body and spirit needs.

"What makes it taste good?"

"Taste and see that the Lord is good!"

"Yes, I know that." So I just took a bite. The angels made it. I asked, "How do you make it?"

"Just stack it on top of each other," the angels said. But, mine didn't look as good as theirs. You could see the word underneath. There are only three ingredients. The frosting is PEACE. JOY is what you feel after you eat it. And, LOVE is what makes JOY. You can't have JOY without LOVE. You will not be happy if you don't feel LOVE. They all work together. These are keys.

He took me over the hill where people are always hugging, to His little cabin. He showed me. .He unlocked a drawer, and it wasn't full of clothes, but keys. It was weird because He had given me three, but they were still there.

He said, "You have to know this is possible." When He gave me the keys—in the doll's dress—there was a key-shaped hole for the keys to drop in. I pointed to the yellow one. People say, "PEACE is very yellow, on earth." That's because it is—in Heaven.

The last key is the key of the Holy Spirit. It looks the same as the key of the spirit. They are different though. The Holy Spirit has a name given when Jesus went down. .JOY (H)AM. He's a son. And people in Heaven call Him by that name. It means 'Beautiful Joy'

"Where do you keep all your clothes?" I asked, because He is always in different outfits. "Do angels slip them on you, and we don't see them do it?" It's like it happens when He says something.

"Not exactly," He said. "But JOY-HAM does it."

I asked about another key. He said, "This is the key of your natural body, that unlocks and puts you into your spirit. But because it's used for the natural realm."

There are so many keys. I asked about another one. "This key has never been used on the earth, because people haven't believed yet. When you speak it, it makes nature go along with what you say." It's a key of the spirit realm, because of how it's used. But, because it's used for the natural realm, it's called the Nature Key.

On the other side of the cabin, it was a drop-off. He said, "Step off the rock." I forgot that in Heaven, we can fly, so it looked scary—like natural realm. I stepped off. I flew across to a little path, getting higher.

"Where am I going?" I went through a sliding door that opened as I was sliding down the hill.

People looked surprised. I said, "Who are you?"

"We are the angels without wings."

"But, I thought all angels have wings!" Some are not born with wings and when they grow up—fast—except some who aren't supposed to grow up, they have funny outfits like maids, like cartoon outfits! Why?

"We are made for children. We go down, and get picked back up, since we can't fly." Heaven is in different parts. Jesus is low and high. The Father is up very high. Angels are in different places. I remember seeing the angels without wings in Heaven, singing, when I was a baby and didn't know what I was seeing.

Angels with wings make people happy and change their hearts. Angels without wings, called people angels, do miracles—all different kinds. Some of them have wings, but can't use them. It just makes them look like angels, called Impossible Angels. They work together.

My angel, Lovely, never flies. Now I know she is 'Impossible Angel' a nickname given by people. The angel that told me didn't know what they're called.

"When do they go down?" You have to close your eyes to see them.

FEBRUARY 8

I was in a circle room. As I walked around, I started to laugh and sing. Then I went out to the room where I normally meet Jesus—one of the Love Rooms.

Jesus blinked at me which means, "Come with Me!" He does that sometimes! I don't know why. I walked with Him to this room. .I don't know what it's called.

"What room is this?" I asked.

"This is the Tea Party Room." It was beautiful, but I couldn't see the table. But I saw tea cups with 'Jesus' written on, and each cup had a different picture of Him—like a different outfit.

He said, "Sit down."

I didn't see any chairs, but as I sat down there were two chairs—one for me and one for Jesus. As we drank, He asked me a couple questions. I answered and asked Him questions. I don't remember what.

Then He gave me a tiny box. It was a ring! "But I already have my wedding ring!" I said.

Jesus said, "This is your Friend Ring."

As soon as I put it on, things Jesus had spoken over me went into the ring. Day after day, I have been wearing my wedding ring, and checking if anything would show up on it.

Now when He gave me the Friendship Ring is the first time anything showed. I saw some little kids on the ring. He said, "Do you remember those two little kids—where it was about freedom for America?"

"I met them, but I didn't really know their names." The kids, a boy and a girl were playing freedom in all countries of the world. They weren't from any particular country—like they didn't know what country they were from. They live on the earth, but their spirits are in Heaven also.

Then I saw Jesus and me dancing in a field. I took His Hand, and I did dance. And for the first time, I kissed Him on His cheek!

That was the end!

FEBRUARY 9

Rachel and I talked this morning about our angels. As I was describing my experience of meeting my two angels—how Sarah was like someone I had always known, and how I laughed in surprise when I met Maggie—Rachel interrupted me. .

"Yes, Sarah is your mother angel, and Maggie is your joy angel. Everybody has first a mother angel who cared for you in Heaven before you came down. And, the second angel is the joy angel. Everybody needs to laugh!"

I definitely knew in my spirit these two were chosen for me. I was filled with gratitude, a fresh appreciation for Father who knows what I need much better than I. Years ago, during a period of deep discouragement, I had found Hebrews 11:11—Sarah's miracle faith to bring forth the promised Son. And, I have never let go. He had given Helpers long before I recognized my need or their presence. Sarah is on my right, and Maggie on the left. And I once caught a glimpse of Simon, our finance minister, carrying the money bag. I am hoping to be aware of them and cooperate with them more and more.

I started thinking about a ladder or stairs, to Heaven. And after we had talked about it, I read it, heard it in a message, read it by Chuck Pierce and

David Herzog that day and the next. So, I caught myself 'running up' several times. I am being so affected by the open Heavens, as a child leads the way. I am in awe. .of the nearness, the reality, the simplicity of access, found by a child.

FEBRUARY 11

I was in Heaven, and I saw Jesus. He gave me a big kiss.

"That's the first time You kissed me!" I said.

In this room was a lot of happy crying, clapping, and more. "What is happening that is so good here?"

Jesus said, "On earth they got healed, and have never been sick since. And others just because of my Love. There were three who got their minds healed."

"You mean I was one of the three!?"

He said, "You were one. . after it happened, there were three who were crying because they just found out about my love."

There were also three clapping. . brains healed. On earth, it's like the body—they put on a big show in your body! It probably doesn't say that in the science books, but it actually happens. Science probably won't ever find it out (smile).

I was one of the three clapping, and one of the three with a mind getting healed. Until we get to know His Love, our emotions are always sad.

But, it wasn't really sad in their spirit. . because of His Kisses, His Love. It was sad in their emotions, in their natural mind. They feel partly both. But in Heaven there aren't emotions—like sad or angry. There is only happiness.

Jesus said, "If you close your eyes, you will see Me kissing everyone in the line!" Twirling in the dance, Mommy was first in line, and I was last. I didn't know anyone else.

Later, when I took a nap during worship, I saw this. "Jesus, why was I at the last of the line?"

"Because your Mom needed it most and you the least."

I gave Jesus a really big hug. Then we danced. . in a tiny room. It was a waltz, and I wondered if I would bump the wall. I did end up doing that. But there was no pain. Mommy kept dancing with Jesus, and said, "I will never let go!"

I wondered, why did she say that?

"Didn't you see on the earth realm how she turned the hook?" He said. "On the earth realm, she will never experience stress, or sadness, or ever anger again. Only happiness!

I said the same thing as I also was giving Him a hug.

So, if it ever did start to happen, we just come back to the vision and hold on to Jesus again. Sometimes, by mistake, on the earth, it is easy to let go.

So, even though I don't feel good today, I am still actually holding on to His Hand. I've been thinking about it all day. . because it was a wonderful vision. I wasn't just napping. I was resting and holding on to the vision all day.

It was a WONDERFUL vision! It was a WONDERFUL dream!

It was together, but somehow connected with the earth realm. I don't know exactly.

> "Until we get to know His Love, our emotions are always sad. "

FEBRUARY 17

I was in Heaven and saw a giant hill—like a mountain size. I was going along, over to the side where you could climb up. It didn't take long at all to get to the top.

Jesus said, "You've been here before." I didn't think so. It wasn't very recognizable. "It was where you slided down the other side, and were crying and crawling up to Me."

It seemed impossible, but of course it isn't. It just seems BIG, and it's your first time. When you get to the top it doesn't look so big.

"Where are you taking me?" I grabbed His hand. He was just silent. By the time we were on the other side of the hill, I asked why He didn't answer. He said, "Can't you believe my surprises happen all the time?"

"Yes, I do."

"My surprises just happen sometimes—without saying, 'Come with Me' or anything. Can you also believe that?"

When God made the earth, He had to speak it. So it didn't make much sense to me.

"It came that way, when I came to earth. ." He usually talks in ways I can understand. Now it doesn't make much sense, but I still believe.

I said, "OK." And I walked with Him. There was a waterfall, and a Heaven rainbow. . water splashing. . not magic. But rainbows happen after God walks by—after the splash. We walked on the bridge.

"Why do we have bridges in Heaven, if we don't need them?" I asked.

It's like on earth—there are people who don't believe they can fly. People weren't made just to walk.

Mama: !!! I'm so glad to hear that! It explains why the majority of children who are asked what animal they would be if they could choose, choose birds! Hey! I'm ready to sign up for the real flying lessons!

"I fly, so you can too!" He said.

I guess the reason it doesn't happen is because people don't believe. It seems impossible because of gravity, and everything. But people can do it—if they believe. You might not know it's happening. It seems they're too heavy, so they just jump around. (I'm talkin' earth here.) People have wings they don't know about. People think it's only in dreams. But you can do anything if you only believe.

"So where are we going?" I asked. We ended up at this place that looked like a weird-shaped castle. "I've been to the Castle of Love, but what is this?"

"You know that you're princesses, but do you know that you're also kings and queens?" Jesus was talking about each of us.

"This is where I used to rule until I moved to the lower part where people are that don't come up to higher places. So now this is for my other kings and queens."

"How many are there?!"

"I can't even explain how many there are!" Jesus said.

My next question was, "Where is my crown?" I have never seen myself with a crown!

"People picture Me with a crown in Heaven, but I really never had a crown. The only thing crowns are for is for people to know who is the king. Everybody in Heaven knows who I am."

"Why are the thrones empty?" There aren't many people that know about it. You don't sit until you know about it. In other countries they have to become Christians.

"People said You died with a crown. Why?"

"A crown of thorns isn't really a crown. In Heaven a crown is what you believe." Then He said, "You will get yours now."

On a little table there were some crowns—with fruits, favorite verses, earth and Heaven fruit—like Love, Joy. . and pictures of the person (me) with Jesus. "I never saw angels taking pictures with a camera!"

"No, we don't need that in Heaven."

So I put mine on, and sat on the throne that had my name—Diamond—that's what He calls me. I was surprised that it was comfortable, because wood doesn't seem comfortable—even painted.

Jesus said, "Touch it."

It was soft like a carpet, but of wood? I just sat there not doing anything. Then, I hugged Jesus and that was the end.

FEBRUARY 19

I was in Heaven and I saw something very bright. I kept looking at it but I didn't know what it was. When I got closer, I saw it was Jesus. I never saw Him like that—sort of round.

He said, "Today and three more days you will see a review of what you've seen before, of Heaven. Do you remember when you went through the History Room? You will go through the History Room and the Future Room." It always has new things to see.

So in the History Room, I started in the New Testament—not the Old like I would have thought. I saw Mary and Joseph. Mary was walking the whole way to Bethlehem. The time she saw the angel—when she prayed—the angel talked in the Jewish language.

Mary said, "It will happen! Oh thank you, Lord! Thank you, Lord!"

Nobody was really helping Mary when Jesus was born. I think it was about three days after they got there. Then I saw Jesus when He was twelve, and they found Him in The Temple. Mary said, "We were so worried about you."

Jesus said, "I do my Father's work."

In the History Room, it skips parts—like when He was five—probably to just the most important parts? Then His first miracle at the wedding. Everyone was invited. They ran out of wine. Mary was sitting in this little place on the grass. And she whispered to Him, "Can't you do something?"

He answered, "It's not my time yet."

Then Mary said to a servant, "Do whatever my son tells you."

He said, "Get ten. . pots? Containers?—filled with water." I don't know what they called them, but they were BIG!

They took them to start putting into cups. When they saw it was wine, they were so surprised, they dropped the cups. Actually they dropped, they fell down—which is what happens. I just didn't know it happened back then!

"This is the best wine we have ever tasted! Usually the last isn't as good as the first. But this is better!"

So I said to all of them, including Jesus, "Why is this whole entire wedding in the grass?" It wasn't in a building.

Jesus said, "Because it's tradition. The only time they use a building is Passover." It was small, like a house, but it was called a building.

When we came out of the History Room I said, "How can You be in there, and be here too?"

He said, "I go in when you go in. I go with you, you just don't know it."

I said, "Angels have acted out a play."

But He said, "They won't be doing that much anymore. This year they will be doing a different play. It will be about the future."

I thought that seemed strange, because they like the history. But, we will like it anyway. They do it on our Christmas Eve, when they celebrate Jesus coming back to Heaven—after He brought an end to evil on The earth.

They call it Victory Eve, before Victory Day. So, they do the play on Victory Eve to be ready for the big celebration on Victory Day. . just once a year, which doesn't make sense when you don't have 'Time' in Heaven. But, all there is – is future and history. There isn't 'Right Now'.

A Mama/Rachel discussion led us to decide History and Future is NOW in the Heaven realm!

I didn't go in the future Room. Probably it's because it's not time to see my own future. "When will I see my future?" was my question.

> *I said, "How can You be in there, and be here too?" He said,*
> *"I go in when you go in. I go with you, you just don't know it."*

Jesus said a long time ago, "When you see the second time the New Testament History , you'll see your future." So, I'll probably see it one of these three days.

<u>FEBRUARY 20</u>

I was in Heaven looking down on earth in the spirit realm. I saw not just stars and moon, but an angel coming down to the earth from the high part of Heaven. People are partly right when they think Heaven is far away—the high part.

I said to Jesus, who was right next to me, instead of an angel. "Why is the angel coming down?"

He said, "She is to show herself to a little girl." I forgot her name. She wanted to see an angel. She had seen Jesus on the earth right next to her. And she didn't care if she saw an angel in the spirit realm or vision or not. She just wanted to see one.

I've heard of Gabriel, but I didn't know if this was the same Gabriel. There are two, a man and a woman angel, that came to Mary. When they have the same name they do something the same.

This little girl was four. And four years old don't usually remember seeing Jesus. I often ask them in Heaven.

"But I remember You!"

He said, "You are older, but you did see Me when you were four, and didn't remember—didn't tell your mom." When it's God who gives you dreams it's easier to remember.

He said, "Come with Me," 'cuz I've already seen all this. We went back to the Castle Throne Room. I saw a big chest box.

"What is this?" It wasn't there before, or I didn't see it.

He opened the box and all the jewelry! ! ! "Its all yours!" There was a ring. "But, I already have two!" I said.

"This one is for remembering an angel friend that you may have forgotten—different at different times. Some that met me the first time to Heaven, I have forgotten. "Who was sitting in the chairs that first time?"

Jesus said, "One was Flowers."

"Why Flowers?" I asked. "Does she smell like flowers?"

"No, it's like people say, 'You're as sweet as a flower!' 'As wonderful as a flower!' 'Sweet like honey!'" I think it's a nick-name.

Another was Silly Laughy Angel to help make you laugh. Baby angels do that too (my Baby Laughy).

Jesus said, "You were given two angels to make you laugh, both for different times." Laughy looks like she's laughing when she worships, but she doesn't make me laugh.

I never told you about a holiday in Heaven. It's just angels' Joke Day. They do jokes to make you laugh, like knocking on your door when it sounds like two angels, but it's just one. It's on a day when you're sad, or really need to laugh.

Right now I laughed because I remember how Lovely knocks REAL LOUD!

When you see some light when there aren't lights turned on, it's Jesus or angels. It's a different and sparkly light.

Sometimes I'm not sure if the knocks are people, or angels when I don't know it. Sometimes I'm playing and hear a knock. When I go to the door, there is no one there. So maybe it is an angel.

FEBRUARY 21

I was in Heaven and I saw Jesus with something in His Hand. "What is in your hand?" I asked.

"It is oil."

I said, "What are you thinking. . oil in your hand?!!"

Jesus said, "When people in the Bible get anointed to be the King. It's time for you to be anointed."

I guess it happens after you already are king or queen. "Won't this burn my body?"

"No," He said, "this isn't regular oil. This is Heaven's Joy oil." Then, He poured it on my head.

85

I started laughing, and I realized it was joy oil! "Where do you get the oil?"

"I'll show you."

Then me and Jesus went to this place with rainbows and butterflies. "Welcome to the room of hearts and rainbows!" Angels named the room, but I didn't see any hearts.

Jesus said it makes your spirit feel so WON-der-ful when you're in there! It's the only room I've seen with a window.

"Why is there a window here?" I think angels mostly use it to look into the room. "How did all these buildings get built?"

He said, "They didn't get built. I just spoke it for them to be here."

I said, "Where is the oil I've been waiting to see?"

Over on the left, there was a box, a crate, that Jesus opened. There was lots of oil—the Joy Oil, Oil of Heaven—used only for earth, others used only in Heaven or both, and Oil of Heart. Jesus said this is very old and has only been used once. It was just a little bit of it in God's mouth when He made people (Adam) and He spit on the dirt.

"So why do you still have it?"

Jesus said, "We will end up using it again. I don't know when. No one knows."

The last bottle was Oil of Everything. "How is it different from the Oil of Heaven?" If you know about the oils, but don't have much belief, you could use Oil of Everything.

FEBRUARY 22

I was in Heaven and saw Jesus again. "Where are you taking me today?"

"Come with Me," He said.

I went with Him, and He said, "Come closer to Me." I was only a step from Him, but He wanted me to come closer.

"I've never been in this place. Where is this?"

He said, "This is the River of Everything!"—of Love, Joy—being alone with Jesus—and Peace. These are just some examples.

It was just so wonderful. . feelings wise. . not the way it looked. I sat there with Jesus (there were places to sit).

"By the next night you'll see all of Heaven, all angels, all the people dancing and celebrating."

"Why are you celebrating?" I asked.

Jesus said, "We do this all the time—not when people are watching. Angels don't want people to be too, too surprised. It's OK if they are a little surprised."

Jesus gave me a ring—the Story Ring—all the stories in the Bible. You can choose your favorite and click on it. Everything-in-Heaven, pictures and writing, is pretty tiny. Nothing is big. Angels must want to test your Heaven eyes! With earth eyes it would look like a dot of paint!

Jesus also said a long time ago that before He comes back, painters on earth will paint so small that normally your earth eyes wouldn't be able to see it. But you and your family will be able to see it.

I said, "I already know my favorite story!" and I clicked on it.

And then we started dancing in the room. I gave Him a big hug. Then Jesus gave me my memory book. I've been waiting a long time to get it. It was huge. It held so many pictures and things.

"I don't think it will fit in my box!"

Jesus said, "There's a button on it that makes it the size of a regular book—to fit into the box. Then when you take it out, it becomes really big."

Then I said 'good bye' to Jesus. I don't know why, because He's everywhere. I guess because I was leaving. I went to my room where my box was, with jewelry and special things, and put my book in it.

Then I went back to Jesus. And He gave me a flute. It made music when I played it, But it didn't make a song? Why?

Jesus said, "It IS a song. But for people who are just visiting Heaven it's hard to learn the song. And hard to remember when you wake up."

Then I put that in my music box.

It was a dream of WONDERFUL FEELING. IT WAS FRIENDSHIP TIME WITH JESUS !

FEBRUARY 24

We just returned after a week away to see how much Rachel remembers of her Heaven journeys! She says she remembers every night! Wow! "Well, Rachel, where do we start?"

We'll start with the day you left. I was in Heaven, and I saw Jesus and this beautiful 'something'—like a rose petal. But Jesus said it wasn't. "Have you looked up at the trees?" He asked.

The leaves were like giant rose petals, that also smelled like roses. They were to eat and they tasted good. This was the only tree that I've seen in Heaven that doesn't grow fruit. Jesus said, "These are fruit leaves. They are fruits of the Spirit, though they don't look like fruits."

"What fruit of the Spirit is this?" I asked.

"Can you guess?" He said. I guess He thought I would know.

"Wait!" I said. "Who would you give a rose petal to, unless you loved them?!" (smile)

"You guessed it! It's the Tree of Love. Climb up there."

My answer was kind of a weird one. I said, "I don't know how to climb."

Jesus said, "In Heaven you can do anything. You just don't know you can."

On earth, only one or two people could sit in a tree. In Heaven, you can fit one hundred or even maybe a thousand. Jesus climbed up with me. He just started speaking out things to me. He usually does not do that in Heaven. He only speaks when I or other people ask Him questions.

He started talking about things that will happen on earth soon. He didn't say how soon. The first thing He mentioned was that you will be able to fit the same amount of people in a tree on earth as you would in Heaven.

That's not what I picture. I picture healing people, Jesus on the earth, the whole entire earth being pretty. . Heaven on earth. But, I didn't say that. Then Jesus explained—wanted me to know—it's going to be better than I think.

In your spirit it will be soon, but outside that, it seems longer—like even a few years. The other thing Jesus mentioned was that there will be like little tiny cabin parts "for just you and Me." In Heaven right now there is only one, but on earth there will be many.

Jesus doesn't talk much about the future. Only sometimes He does. He wants you to know everything is NOW! NOW! NOW! He said, "Meet Me at this tree tomorrow, and every day for two weeks. If you meet Me any place else, I will not talk about the future."

"Why?"

"Because this is the only place that people don't come and sneak in here to hear. A lot of people from the Bible would understand, but not others" (because their minds have messed them up).

He has talked to people in the Bible. I was in Christ, so I was in the Bible. A lot know that they are in Christ, the Hope of Glory. There are people there that don't know—in their natural body, or in their spirit—that they are in Christ. They are there to learn. Some of them are damaged in their mind. Then the bad stuff goes in their spirit, and partly damages their spirit.

Jesus says He will fix their spirit completely (he fixes by just passing by them). But many of them just don't catch it. They mostly get it on earth by a dream, or someone just healing them. Probably this is why Jesus wants me to write these dreams.

So, He will fix their spirit completely. And, if they believe it's real—what He fixes in their spirit—then it will fix their mind. But, it doesn't always happen, because they don't think it's real. Their mind has to catch the message from their spirit.

The way to catch it is to close your eyes, and be in the spirit, or speak in tongues for a while, or just start laughing outloud. It works different ways for different people. For me, it's laughing a lot—not just cause something is funny. I feel like angels tickling me or whisper something in my spirit ear. And my natural body gets it, and it makes me laugh. I feel it all the time, but I don't do it in front of people much. They would think I'm crazy. I do it with my friends. They don't think I'm crazy. And, I do it alone, or playing outside.

I say all my fears are gone *(We definitely notice a difference here—since last year when her 'mind got fixed')*. But, that's my only one that has stayed. He has been fixing that part, but I have to adjust to it. I'm having trouble with that. But, when I adjust, I will be laughing everywhere—except on stage—unless I'm supposed to! *(Rachel had recently been in local kids' theatre!)*

People who don't know Jesus mostly don't catch it, cause their minds are filled with the world—UNLESS they are children. When I come down from the spirit into the natural, and I asked them, they say, "Yes, we do understand." Or, they say, "I catch God's voice." (If it's really bright when you go down, it's usually the spirit realm. But, sometimes it's not bright, and it's the natural realm.)

The only thing I want to change with the dreams is to not change to the morning dreams (earth dreams, and silly dreams). I want to continue all night, and remember right away when I wake up. I don't know when it will happen, or if I need to do something different. He told me "Soon." But, that was when I was seven, and I asked Him. The remembering part is fixed, but the morning dreams—I'm wondering if it is something I'm thinking that needs to change.

> *"Jesus doesn't talk much about the future. Only sometimes He does. He wants you to know everything is NOW! NOW! NOW!"*

FEBRUARY 25

I was in Heaven at the tree, and Jesus was in the tree with me. I didn't have to find the place, or climb, which was new thinking to me, just being there.

"Why did You talk to me about the future, when I didn't ask You anything?"

"I've been doing this for four years," He said. "And you have been doing it with me."

"I don't remember doing it."

Jesus said, "You wouldn't remember. You were very young."

"How young?" I asked.

"You were one year old."

"But, I don't think I had any dreams when I was one."

He said, "Yes, you had dreams when you were very little. But when you got older, everything changed."

"Why did everything change?"

He said, "A two-year-old is the same as a five-year-old."

"What do you mean?"

He said, "I mean that first of all, babies know Heaven language. It's a different kind of language." Jesus explained that "Da-da-da" is saying something to Jesus, or to his brother or sister. A baby only knows his family in the natural. In his spirit, he only knows Jesus, and the angels, and stuff around Heaven. As he grows, he learns to know everyone—in his spirit.

I wondered, "How do they switch around?"

All babies know Jesus, or give their heart, so you could say they're Christian. But, as they grow, they give it up for a while. Then they switch back, and give back with Him.

"But why do they give it up?" Even in the spirit realm, that doesn't make sense to me. He is the most Wonderful Guy in the world!

"Some babies must feel they are there all the time. But, as they are surrounded by their family, and hear them, they lose the feeling, and lots of them go away."

The good part is that lots of them come back. When I came back to the Lord, my whole mind didn't change. I kept part of my mind in place—stuck. And some things are still getting out of there.

I had dreams from Heaven, but I could still easily get tricked. I think all people can get tricked.

Now that my mind is fixed, I don't get tricked any more. I know His Voice very well. You can know God's voice, but the other voice sounds ALMOST like God's voice. Even though the devil is dead—has no power, he has the power to trick you. It's the only power he has.

I said to Jesus, "When will you—You finished the work—so when will you take away all the 'overdraft'?—the stuff all around my mind!"

"It's not my stuff to take away. It's your job to believe, and keep your mind fixed on what its fixed on."

"How will I do that? How will I keep it that way?" I asked.

Jesus said, "If you can keep your mind focused on Me."

"But there are times when things pop into my mind."

He said, "It pops in, but, it's because you're not always focused on

Me—but on the world. So, take that side of your brain off. . both sides cut off, and then put them back together. Fix it altogether."

It's like He said about the hand that you cut off one side. It's not trying, or working; it's thinking in your mind.

We were both on natural earth by now. "Jesus," I said crying, "I try so hard to keep my focus. How can I do this?"

"You don't need to TRY. Your focus is always there. You just need to know it." He was trying to explain it. . until the end of the dream. He didn't say anything else. The whole time, He was trying to say I just have to believe. I was having a hard time to understand.

"Why did you say it in a way that was hard to understand?" I asked.

He said, "I'm giving you a challenge to understand. I'm giving your mouth, your ears, your mind, a challenge to get it. I didn't say TRYING, and never getting it. I'm saying to BELIEVE."

But, He sometimes speaks in ways that challenge your mind, ears, body, to know what He's saying. He will explain it in the end—if you don't understand. This is new to me—to hear Him talking in ways I don't understand.

This was a dream that people won't understand, until they get to the end. It was almost like He was talking like I should try harder. But He wants us to know we should just focus on Him, and believe.

It was the first time He made me cry with what I thought He was saying. But, He was trying to say, "NEVER GIVE UP ON BELIEVING!" I think it's a message for many people. They give up on believing.

FEBRUARY 26

I was in Heaven at the tree. I climbed up and Jesus said, "It won't be just cabins, but Heaven mountains to climb that lead to high parts of Heaven. Heaven will be everywhere by that time.

So, there will be mountains—just places to be with Jesus, (not just mountains to go up to high places).

People will know about their spirit, and know that they are alive. They will experience the Heavenly realm all the time. I feel Heavenly places and angels all around my body. In a couple years everybody will experience Heaven just in their body. Outside their body comes later, when nature will go along with it. I don't know how long is a couple years.

Our animal for our country is an eagle. In Heaven their 'pet' is a gold eagle. If you see it in an earthly place with your natural eyes, then it's very close, very soon. Jesus said He doesn't know exactly when. I see it in Heaven, but I haven't seen it yet with my natural eyes.

"When? Jesus! When?!"

Jesus said, "I don't know. But, it's your job to speak the good news or write it, to other peoples in the world. It's my job to help them understand."

It's not like a working thing. It's a fun job. He said, "Take your string and pull it."

> *"He was trying to say, "NEVER GIVE UP ON BELIEVING!"*
> *I think it's a message for many people. They give up on believing."*

I said, "What does that mean?"

"That means take what you have in your spirit, by speaking in tongues, or worshipping. And when it gets in your mind, pull the rope, and spread it all around the world. You don't have to go all over the world speaking. You can do it right here in worshipping and speaking."

I knew that. But, I hadn't been using my 'Encouraging Book' for a long time. "When will I use it again?"

Jesus said, "I have some plans, but it won't happen until after these two weeks. You'll still see me after three months, but you will be with the angels."

Why are You changing it back?" 'Cuz that's the way it used to be.

"There are some things I show you that angels can show you, as well. They aren't just for helping rescue people on earth."

"Then, why don't YOU show me?"

Jesus said, "It's mainly because. . angels don't miss anybody, but they have little surprises that the Heavenly Father gives them for you."

Then why doesn't the Heavenly Father show me?"

"He loves you, but He can't show you in a way that you can understand. When He talked to Me in the Bible, I could understand, but the people couldn't. So I said it in a different way—that they could understand."

In my natural body, I wouldn't be able to understand what Jesus says, or what the Father says. Jesus said they speak in Heavenly language, and

I'm still learning. He said He will teach me half of earth languages. But, I don't know how many that is.

So the angels help us understand. Some angels never come down to earth. They are 'Understanding Angels.'

"Why did you make Understanding Angels?"

"I didn't. My Father did. The day He created light, there were angels in Heaven."

So—I didn't know there were no angels before He created the earth. But, I knew there were angels before He created man. I don't know why, but it was the same day as Light.

I asked how many songs there are in Heaven. He said, "There are a lot more in Heaven than on earth. You are not only a bookwriter, but a songwriter." He sees me in the future.

He said, "You'll always be a kid, and you are writing now. But, you will write songs that go with the dreams. You are the one to fill up songs in Heaven to bring them to earth. People need them." Then there will be more songs on earth than in Heaven.

"Why do you give me dreams that I don't understand? Mainly the one that makes me laugh."

"That's the only one you don't understand. It's just to make you laugh!"

> "Jesus said, ". .it's your job to speak the good news, or write it,
> to other peoples in the world. It's my job to help them understand."

FEBRUARY 27

I was in Heaven, and I saw Jesus in the Tree. He said, "Come up to the top." We were sitting in the middle. So I was looking down on all other trees and stuff, and people with baskets. It wasn't on earth.

"Who are these people?"

"They are angels with baskets, getting ready for the feast. Did you know there is a celebration—like Passover, but just with wine and fruit, not with bread. It comes this time of year, but not always the same day. The angels plan it. And it's for all of Heaven."

When I went down to them, I saw that they had wings. They were hidden. Not all angels have wings. Jesus asked if I wanted to go to the feast. Of course I did. And, when we got close, I saw all the fruit that was picked.

Fruit from the Tree of Life

Leaves from the Tree of Love

Fruit from the Tree of Peace—tastes like peaches, but way, way better.

The Tree of Joy

The Tree of the Holy Spirit —it is everything that is good for you. Why do we need anything else?!

The Bible Tree—the Word of God for your mind.

The Tree of Glory—all the fruit was glowing very bright.

People in Heaven joke that Jesus has too much glory to fit in His body There were many more fruits I can't remember now, and lots of each kind to share.

In Heaven, you don't plant seeds—except in people's hearts. They just grow up when they speak it. And the angels gave the suggestions about the taste of the fruits. "Why did the angels pick the 27th of February?"

"It's the celebration of when I died, and raised from the dead." That's the best part. They could celebrate all year, but they just pick a day. On earth we always have the same day, but they don't.

> *Makes sense to me since they aren't limited by time and space. We live in eternity now, but our minds have generally been quite limited to time and space.*

How you eat it is, they cut the fruit up like shapes of bread—except for the leaves. Then you eat it with your fingers.

We went back to the tree, and Jesus told me, "The trees that are in Heaven will be on earth. They'll celebrate this celebration every day of the year. It will be a great and wonderful day, and for the angels too. They will be on the earth, and they will be able to see all the people of the earth on the same day! They've never seen that before. And, we will be celebrating the wedding in the future."

Jesus said, "Are you ready to have your 'pretend' wedding?"

It's before the real wedding when Jesus marries everybody. It happens to some—just the ones who die, and are not coming back again. When they first go to Heaven, just alone with Jesus, they do the real wedding.

have been invited to some. They do it in the Ballroom, with lots of angels, and just the people they want to invite.

But, the rest of us do this 'pretend' wedding every year at this feast. I said, "I'm ready!" We went to the place where they were doing it. The angels were singing something very wonderful.

Jesus said, "This wonderful day. . !"

I said, "What are they singing?" Jesus started singing it to me. It was about spirit girl. . like I've heard before. But the angels changed it a little, with so-o-o many verses in Heaven language, so it gives more power to your body.

> To the bride: How beautiful you are.
> How wonderful, wonderful.
> For Jesus: How wonderful Jesus is!
> The Father created.
> He speaks, and everything is made.
> How wonderful! How wonderful You are!

I said, "What a blessing it is to have You with me all the time!"

He said, "It's not much of a blessing."

"It is to me!" I said.

He said, "I had this planned way before you were born. When the earth was made, I had the plan for all the children to see Heaven" (He meant everyone, because everyone is a child).

Then He said, "You chose to keep Heaven with you all the time." I think I'm the third one to see Heaven in dreams, experiencing Heaven staying with me all the time.

"Here comes the pastor!" In Heaven he is the angel called the Pray'er. I said, 'Pastor' 'cuz that's what we call him on earth. Then, I said, "I'm ready!"

We did our 'I Do's' and kissed. And we did a different kind of dancing. A dance I don't know very well, but it's special for that celebration. Jesus told me that someday on the earth, I would be like a back-stage helper of plays—to choose for the director.

When I left, I said, "This is one of the MOST WONDERFUL days in Heaven!"

Jesus said, "You will have many wonderful dreams like this for the rest of your life."

Bride Rachel dancing with Jesus

FEBRUARY 28

When I got there, the angels were singing 'Happy Birthday.' There was a special celebration in Heaven for Great Grampa's birthday (I didn't start at the tree this time, because it was a family celebration).

They celebrate birthdays in little celebrations several times a year. For the real birthday they do a big one. They take away the bridge and jump into the River of Joy. After that they do a ball. And, for girls they have flowers coming down on their heads.

At the Ball, Great Grampa wasn't dancing though. He was playing instruments. I don't know what they were called. But it sounded WON-derful! They ended with angels doing worship, and Grampa and others joining in.

I can't explain how they sing it. But it was wonderful. It was to Jesus. It always is, of course. . to all Three of Them. It's what they always do at the end—for everybody's birthday. At the end, Grampa was laughing and laughing. Lots of people do. It is so wonderful!

The angels don't worship on stage in front of other people ordinarily—except for birthdays. Then there are lots of people who visit from earth, and probably some who live in Heaven. I didn't know any of them. And, I don't know if they were friends of Grampa, or not. But, people are all friends in Heaven, even if they aren't friends on earth.

This one blew me away. We were away on a cruise, and the kids at home with 'sitters'. Rachel did not know that Grampa's birthday was the 28th. He has been in Heaven for a year now. I told her how happy this made me—to know that my Dad, who loved music, was playing WON-derfully—like he always wished! So birthday wishes do come true! Rachel often stops to strum the harp he made, that sits at the top of our stairway I was sure I heard the echoes of his laughter again. It was wonderful! Hmmm. . Heaven really isn't so far away.

March 2013
Age Ten

MARCH 1

I was in Heaven and saw this beautiful, wonderful. . whatever it was. . in the sky! I asked Jesus, "What is this???"

"The Love Sky." He said. "Touch it!"

"I thought, 'Are you crazy?' But I would never say that! It was al spinning and going around like a whirlpool. You would think it would al come down on you if you touched it. But it wouldn't hurt you. It woulc be like you were stuck to the air, or something.

Jesus said, "It's not that scary. Just believe and it will be O.K." He can tell what anyone is thinking even if you didn't say anything with your mouth. So I touched this weird sky. And it became calm, and completely straight. I thought things like that only happen on earth.

Jesus said, "They happen in Heaven too. The reason it happens is sc people don't think that's a crazy sky"—meaning touching it and making it stop.

"You said, 'This is the Sky of Love.' But, I don't feel any extra love, any more than I usually do."

Jesus said, "There is a wonderful place of Love up there. That's Heaven. But no one goes up there. The Father goes, but I don't even know how to get up there."

So, I said, "Jesus, there must be a way."

He said, "I've gone to the High parts of Heaven to see if there is a path. But I have not seen if there is a way." He tries to get up there, but it isn't 'works' (when He tries). He just looks around for a way. His Father was right next to Him. He said, "There must be a way." He asked His Father, "What is the way?"

Father said, "Look closely."

We looked closely, and there was a stairway. I said to myself, "There is another way, but they can only go that way when you see Them as One.

I said, "Let's go up the stairway." We went up. Even though it's high, it only had about three stairs. That seems strange. But in Heaven three stairs can be really high. There were places to sit, places to dance, and there was a place in this room that goes out, and up. So it was a place for picnics. There was a basket to use if anyone wanted to.

So I really did see and feel God's Love up there. Even though I always feel it, up there I REALLY, REALLY felt it.

We had a little picnic. It was the most wonderful food I've ever tasted in Heaven! Then we went back in, and did a little waltz around the fire, and with a CD, which seemed funny. It wasn't electric. It just played when you walked in.

After we were done dancing, Jesus gave me a 'protect' ring to protect your natural body when you go back to earth. And I kinda' feel like I have it on right now. It's supposed to keep you from getting sick, to keep the body from going away from what it was created, to keep the supernatural alive.

Then we went down a slide-way that we had found while we were walking. It was a little far—though everything in Heaven is close. It took us to the place where people come up to the high part—where the mountain is—where I encourage people.

"But, Jesus, we didn't go down to the water, to the rock yet. Who am I encouraging today?"

"Whoever you feel like encouraging," He said. "Whoever you think of."

He gave me a 'help necklace' to use on earth when you really need help. It will catch onto Heaven, and bring down to the low places—whatever you need. You can also use it to keep you from thinking the wrong way.

So I gave Jesus something. I never gave Him something before. I never had anything to give Him. I reached behind my back. It was something we don't have on earth. It was the Faith sword. It's meant for you to keep. But, you give it to Jesus to keep for a little while, because it shows how much you have believed. It's not for work. It's Jesus' kind of surprise to know how much you have believed. It's a good surprise for Him!

Jesus said, "You have believed way more than a lot of people I know." Then He gave it back to me. It's for me to hold onto—to keep on believing.

Then we went down the waterfall to the place where we talk and encourage people in the Heaven way. I didn't think of anyone to encourage. We just sat and talked, though I don't remember much what He said. I said, "I have never imagined You giving me things to use only on earth."

> *"So I gave Jesus something..It was the Faith sword..you give it to Jesus to keep for a little while, because it shows how much you have believed. "*

He said, "I gave you those two things because you will need them a lot of times."

I said, "This is one of the most wonderful times in Heaven I have ever had!"

Jesus said, "Me too."

After a little while, I saw an angel wa-ay down below on the earth. It was weird seeing an angel carrying a flower basket. She was taking it to some girl's mom. The flowers kind of encourage people to do more—not more work—but like spending more time with their children.

In that country—wherever it is, there are guards watching the doors to keep them safe. I think angel guards—to keep people from breaking in. The angel was also there to help. She was like an angel baby sitter, 'cuz the children were pretty little. She helped keep them safe.

The house was really tiny. There was only one room—kitchen, laundry, and bedroom. Their family was only the mom and two kids. I don't know what happened to the dad.

So, that's who I thought to encourage. Even if they have angels, they still might need a little more, from Heaven. So that's who I wrote. The children really knew God, so they received it. I wrote "Your dad is alive, but I don't know where he is."

That was very encouraging to them. And, the next day he came home! He had been searching for gold, and got lost. He had left when the boy turned two. The daughter knew her dad—from the Heaven realm. She knew what he was like, and what he looked like—just from the spirit.

The boy's birthday was December 9. And the dad finally got out of the deep hole some time in February. He was just doing his job, but he sort of got trapped, and couldn't figure how to get out. The mother and father loved each other. But, the father spent more time with the kids than the mother did. So the baby girl was just turning one when the dad came home.

So they had two celebrations—their dad coming home, and baby's birthday. And, every year they celebrate both. Now the boy is around five, and the girl is three or four. I had been seeing back in time. I don't see that very often. So now, he was leaving again—but not for gold.

He believes in Jesus, for sure. But the mom is the only one who doesn't. He searches for people's things that were from years ago, from their family history. It is sort of a dangerous job. Where he was told to go—to another country—wasn't as dangerous as the gold place. But it was very close to a hole. He had to be very careful. It is very deep, and he has to dig with spoons. He leaves in January, the first day of the year. He will be gone at least a year.

I decided to go down to them. The mom was there. The house was a little dangerous. The electric line coming through the roof was going crazy. I asked the mom, "Did this just start happening?"

"No. Year after year it's this way," she said. "And, when we have been touched by electricity, it did not shock us. God protected us."

It is an old house and they couldn't fix it. Now they are not so poor any more, but they still live there. Both of their families believed in God, but the mother just chose not to, I guess. She used to be in church work.

Oh, I just remembered the children's names—Violet and Jesus. They looked like Spanish. But somebody must have come, like a missionary, and taught them English. The children caught on right away, but now they all understand English.

The boy believed God because of his dad. The girl because she remembered from Heaven, maybe. I mainly talked to the mom about Heaven, even though it is hard—weird—to talk to a person who doesn't believe. The baby was too little to tell about her experiences in Heaven, to her mom. So I said, "You're going to get pregnant with a third baby—in about three days."

She said her son when he was two told her she would have two more babies. I think maybe he had a dream. She said, "He told me a little bit about the babies in Heaven. My son said the two others will be girls."

I said, "That's amazing! That he could explain that when he was only two!"

She said, "We knew right when he was about to be born—that he would be a child that was amazing. That's why we decided to name him Jesus."

I asked, "Why didn't you ever believe?"

She said, "I did for a couple years. But after something happened to my brother. . I had four brothers and two sisters. It was not meant to happen. When he was grown up, he was a policeman. But, he really always wanted to be a pilot. But, he could only find a police job. Then he got shot in the head and died."

So, what she believed didn't happen. I encouraged her by saying, "Do you believe in being raised from the dead?"

She said, "Yes."

I said, "He's not buried, because years ago before your husband married you, he healed a lot of people, and raised them from the dead. And one of them was him. He is alive, but I don't know where, or what he is doing."

Then that instant she got a call from her mom. She had been healed, and got her youth back! (I hadn't seen that before in the earth—that people who worked miracles and raising the dead ever gave their youth back.) Her mom said, "I just got a call from your brother! He's alive! He's working! And, he's flying to Africa as the pilot!"

"What?" She said. "He didn't even have training to be a pilot!"

Her mom said, "They needed pilots, and he had gotten trained." But, she didn't know how he was alive. They lived very far away from each other.

Then she told her mom, "I've just been told that my husband many years ago prayed for people to be raised from the dead. And, one of them was my brother!"

"What?!!" her mom said. "The first time I met your husband, he was preaching and making people walk. I didn't know he was going all over the world, healing and raising people!"

"Mom, you knew my husband before I did?!" she said.

"Yes, he was going to get something to eat, and I was part of the group."

Then the daughter said, "How did you know he would be my husband?"

Her mom said, "When I talked to him, I knew you would marry him. God told me he was the kind of man you would need. And, here we are—twenty seven years later—and you are still married to him. You believe different things, but you are still together. You have two beautiful children, and another on the way soon. A Christian friend said, 'Your daughter is going to be pregnant—in three days.'"

Reminder: Three Heaven days is three months on earth.

I said, "Your mother knew a lot about you that she wouldn't naturally know."

She said, "My mother told me what you and my son told me."

Then I stayed for three months with them. The father came home. And later when the baby came, guess who came to the hospital? The brother pilot! He was flying missions, and regular job-pilot. She said to her brother, "I got a call three days ago from Mother, and she got her youth back!"

"Yes, I know!" He said. "She told me too."

"Now here I am today, having a new baby! So cute!" The baby was named 'Believer' because she believed before she got pregnant. They are a happy family. They took many pictures of Believer. She takes the pictures with her everywhere—to remind her of when she first believed. She goes with her brother once in a while to other parts of the world.

Is this a family we will meet someday? Or, is it many different people and situations, or maybe both?

MARCH 2

I was in Heaven with Jesus. I don't know where. So I said, "Jesus, where are we?"

"Don't you reco-nise this place?" He asked.

"No, not really." I said.

Then Jesus said, "You've been here the first time when you were a baby and couldn't explain to your mom."

And the second time was when I could explain a little bit. But, it was a long time ago, so I didn't recognize it. It looks different when you're older.

There are two throne rooms—one for everybody to come. The other one is just for Jesus and whoever wants to sit with Him. I was in the second one and I saw a river that looked like honey. But Jesus said it was a river of glory. I wouldn't have known because it didn't light up at all like glory usually does.

I said, "How does this work?"

He said, "There isn't a way it works. It just works!" It's the same with trees. It isn't how it works. It just works!

"What does it do?" I asked.

Jesus said, "Touch it and you will see!"

I touched it, and started to feel light. I can't explain how glory feels. It's just so wonderful! I didn't only feel it on me, but I felt it was on the natural earth all the time. I said to Jesus after it happened, "How did that just happen?" (I only felt it for about three minutes.)

Jesus said, "No one knows how my glory works, and how it happens. It just works by itself, and by its power in you."

That was just one of the most wonderful times I've had in Heaven; and it was just one little part of my time there. I asked, "Where are your disciples living now, in Heaven?"

"They are living in Me—just like you are," He said. "All disciples are, as I told you a long time ago."

Then I went back over to where I felt the glory. And the rest of the dream was me just sitting there. . being in the glory.

MARCH 3

I was in Heaven, and I saw something that looked a tiny bit like a boat. "What is this?"

Jesus said, "It's a water scene."

"Why would there be a picture of water and a boat in Heaven?" I asked. It was about the disciples after Jesus had finished speaking and said, "Take me out into the deep."

He said, "The angels, boy angels, will be acting out this story in about three days." That would be on Mama's birthday, which I didn't know at the time, until Heather told me later. The angels only need to practice a couple times, and they get it right. It's not like on earth, where we have to practice a lot.

"Where do they practice?"

He said, "Pretty much everywhere—anywhere they can."

"Where do they start?" I asked.

He said, "Different times at different places."

"Where today?" I asked.

Jesus didn't know. Angels like to practice alone. But they don't get stage fright. In Heaven you're not afraid of anything. And lots of times, only a couple people come to see the show.

We went to the place where I encourage people and just talked together. Hardly anybody comes there, unless they are new in Heaven. It's in the high parts of Heaven, but not the high, high part. We asked each other questions. Even though Jesus knows everything about me. But He asked anyway, and I answered. Of course, I always ask questions! I don't remember what.

One question I asked, "What is going on down there?"—because the mountain was shaking, and I never felt that before.

Rachel and Jesus on the mountain top

He said, "The mountain shakes like that when the River is coming down close to the earth. You have not felt it before because you normally come here when the river is going slow. A lot of people feel this—a good feeling—the mountain shaking though it's not an earthquake. Something good is happening on the earth."

Then we went to the Throne Room that is for all of us. This time instead of most thrones being empty, most of them had people in them. "Why are they full?" I asked. Actually, only one was empty.

He said, "More people have been knowing about it in their hearts (instead of just in their minds)."

I don't know why I had trouble finding mine, because then I found it easily.

When I did, I just enjoyed, basked, in His Presence all night.

I think maybe the change happened in people when the mountain was shaking. That was pretty amazing. I've never known that kind of change before!

March 4

I was in Heaven. I saw Jesus and a beautiful rainbow right above us. I touched the rainbow because I was curious. When I did, everything in Heaven became really colorful. The sky is so close, it's easy to touch rainbows. It was so colorful! I asked Jesus, "What happened?"

He said, "This is how Heaven usually looks. You just haven't seen it this way yet." It was so colorful, and so many colors. I don't know the names of them.

I said, "Jesus, where are we going today?"

He said, "Not anywhere. We are having a picnic right here."

That was different. "Why aren't we going anywhere?"

He said, "Today isn't a day of exploring. It's just a day to stay where you are. The angels are doing that too."

"Why?"

"Every 4th day of March, we just take time with children, when we go to different rooms. I have to think of how to explain things to you. So today we're taking a break from that."

"What are we having for the picnic?" We didn't have a basket. We were just sitting on a blanket, with fruit trees all around, and a rainbow above.

He said, "We'll just pick fruit."

When I picked a fruit, a ring fell out of it! That happens now and then. "What does this mean?"

"That is the ring of glory. You wear it for feeling the Presence of My Glory. You will feel it every day." Then I put it on. And I am still feeling it today (two weeks later). And, I do most all the time.

Then me and Jesus walked through the forest. That is just beautiful all the time. There are weird plants there that sort of look like flowers, or seeds. In the middle, I found some diamonds on the ground, which is not normal for the forest. I have walked before, and found rings. I also found some wooden toys, not to play with, but to play songs like instruments. But, they looked like old wooden toys. I picked some up, and thought I might want to play them sometime.

Jesus said, "What did you find?" (even though He already knew). We were back to the picnic place.

"I found some diamonds, and some instrument things. Why did I find diamonds?!"—which almost never happens.

Jesus said, "Don't you know that when I walk in the forest, things drop off of me for my daughters. Will you play a song?"

"What song?"

"Just play a song that you know."

I don't know many Heaven songs yet. So, I played, "I love you, My Daughter." (*Written in a different book, from a different dream.*)

We relaxed, looked at the rainbow, and, walked around. It was a nice day with Jesus. The 4th of any month is a special rest day with Jesus—starting with March.

MARCH 5

I was in Heaven, and I was told that we are not staying in Heaven for long. We went down, and picked up Mama! She was actually flying with Jesus. We went up into the high parts. I said to Mama, "This is your first time ever being here!" *(Rachel has always called me Mama)*

"Yes!" She said. And the angels started taking her around really fast. They get so excited when it's a grown-up's first time. They show you the lower parts first, then higher and all around—but not in the rooms, except one. It was the 'Meeter Room'. I haven't been in there. They only take people who are first time in Heaven. But I wasn't there, because they usually don't take kids.

Everyone was looking at you, staring at you. The angels don't always know who the grown-ups are. If they don't know your name, they call you Princess. That's what they called me for a while.

You never really talked to the angels. I think you were a little surprised, a little shocked—a good shock. But, you did talk to Jesus. "Where are we going?"

Jesus said, "Wherever you want to go."

You spoke up and said, "The Alone Room" even though you had never been there. It was way down, kind of close to earth. You talked, and Jesus talked, but I wasn't in there with you, so I don't know. . I didn't hear what. At the end, you were given the wedding ring—early, like, way before the wedding, and the Help Necklace (which I was given only a couple days before).

Then the angels showed you your room, where you can go. It's not the only room you have, but you can keep your things—special jewelry, stuff from Jesus—in a box. You can sit on the bed. But, you kept your jewelry.

Interesting! On the cruise, I had been helping my sister shop for special rings. I came home with a desire to add another ring—to stack three 'covenant' rings. One was my grandma's—I wear for my whole extended family. The second was for my children and grandchildren. The third was for thousands of child rescues, orphans and slaves. Tho' I know Heavenly things are different from earthly, maybe the jewelry was inspired from Heaven after all!

When you sat, you looked up so surprised that you were looking at the sky! There aren't windows, because most of Heaven doesn't have ceilings. Your room was up high. I don't know why. My room is in the lower parts. Some people like to be where people are—in the lower parts—people who aren't dead yet.

But, you like to be up with the angels, and where Jesus and God go into each other. So it's usually the Father you see walk up to you. But, you hear Jesus' Voice. And you don't see the Holy Spirit, because He's inside. On the lower parts, you always see them separate.

Jesus and God sound a little bit different, but sometimes God sounds a little bit like people. Jesus sounds calm. God's Voice is more like excited. Jesus' voice is very close to our voice—but not exactly. And He sounds different at different times. Sometimes really, really calm—like whispering.

Yelling is very common in Heaven! I think it started with the angels. There was a time when Jesus was loud, and the angels were quiet! Now they are loud—like almost screaming when they sing. So everyone is loud there.

But you didn't yell; you just talked in your normal voice. The angels did not know what you said. They aren't made to hear quiet voices. But you can't scream at them either. I have a hard time talking to the angels because you have to learn to yell, without being too loud. I usually end up screaming! Ha! With Jesus, He hears any voice.

They want you to have just the right angels to speak to. I have a lot, but they are called 'very few' (??). Angels in lower places can hear different voices better. It was in the high places where the angels are louder. So they couldn't hear you.

But none of those up there were your angels. Your angels talk and hear in a normal voice. I don't normally talk in front of somebody else's angels, (which you would do in the high places. But I don't go there much.) The angels of people on earth live in the lower parts. But, they can take you to the high part, too.

Grampa lives in the lower parts. Gramma had a choice, and she chose to be in the Dancing Room where her Alone Room is. Their rooms are close, and open into the Dancing Room. When Grampa came, he chose to stay with Gramma. They could choose to have their own rooms, or together. They chose together.

Most people chose the high places; but really, you can move any time you choose. Everybody gets to choose how their room looks. The rooms are already decorated. So the angels do a search to find the room of your choice. They found it in the high places.

You chose a room of all Heaven colors. I wanted all the Heaven colors, when I chose my room, too. We don't know what they are. Your bed was Heaven rainbows. They are circles with a lot more than seven colors. On the walls, you wanted pictures of Jesus, and that's what you got! There was a rocking chair, but chairs in Heaven don't look anything like chairs

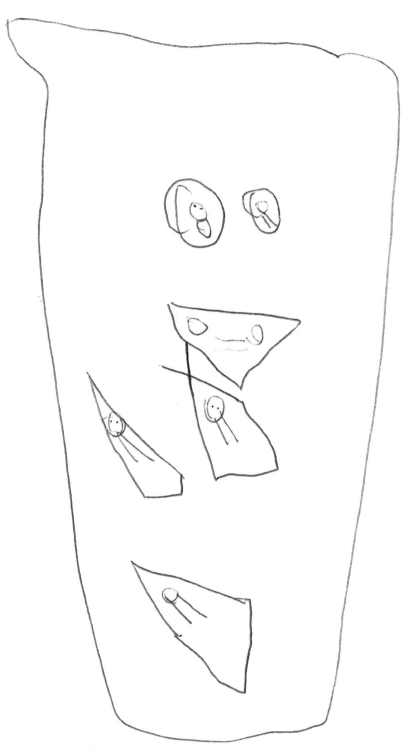

Heavenly hotel room

on earth.

I do like rocking chairs! Did Rachel know that? Probably not.

After a while, you walked around and found the Room of Love. You went in without Jesus—just by yourself. You really felt God's love—a River coming through a crack. You feel it even when you're awake.

In your room there were a lot of Heaven candles that smelled really good.

I love nature smells and pure essential oils. Never thought about Heaven smells. But I did smell a very sweet fragrance once during a group worship time—confirmed by others.

I was somewhere with Jesus, but I don't know what I was doing. I was watching you from the lower parts of Heaven. It's sort of like a hole that you can see and feel what someone is doing in another place.

Jesus came up to you and gave you a hug and kiss, and a box. You would put it in your room to save it for later to open. Most people would open it right away. But you were one of those people who save it for a little later!

I could not have imagined I was going to pick you up that night!

I am just hearing this two weeks after my birthday (March 5), and totally in awe—mostly too precious to share yet—just how specifically and timely Jesus revealed Himself, and me. Present reality of things longed for. In awe of being there when I was not aware!

I had asked Rachel not long ago—when I was saying, 'good night'—"Are you going to take me with you tonight?"

After hesitating, she said, "Mama, it doesn't work that way."

So, I guess that's why she was surprised when it happened. And, then I was surprised that I wasn't 'aware' of it. . but yet. .it is all so familiar. It has opened a new way – in my quest of becoming as aware of Heaven realm, as I am of earth realm 24/7. Oh glorious awakening!

When we got to the part about me saving my treasure to open later, I was laughing. Rachel did not know that's me—since I was a little girl! Just a reminder—there are lots of things in these writings that Rachel does not know from earth knowledge. We, who live with her, can appreciate even more than others, the purity and the wonder of her 'reports'. Now at the time of this printing, Rachel tells me that she always sees me there in Heavenly places. . mainly in my Alone Room!

March 6

I was in Heaven seeing a lot of people looking down in the natura realm, getting healed in lots of different ways. The way they got healed —I don't remember. But, they haven't got sick since then (because it happened a long time ago).

Then I heard a little girl crying and didn't know why she was crying. I went down to her. "Who are you?" I asked.

"I am the daughter of the King, and I am a queen, as well," she said.

"What? You look like a normal little girl!"

And she said, "I'm talking about the spirit realm—not the natural."

"Oh, now that makes sense. Why are you crying?" I asked.

"I don't know why I am crying. But I'm not sad. I just don't know what I'm happy about." Then she said, "I was told to go on-stage to share my testimony, but I'm not afraid. I'm not nervous. Actually it's my mom's testimony. I know she's in this town somewhere. She's not lost, but I don't know where she is."

"Do you know your father?" I asked.

"I know my Heavenly Father, but not my earthly father. I never met him."

Then I said, "You don't need to know him as long as you know your Heavenly Father. He will get everything right." I didn't want to say to a little girl—'You no longer live, but Christ lives in you.' It wouldn't make sense to her. She would think she wasn't supposed to live here.

So, I said, "You are living and Christ lives in you. And you no longer sin."

She said, "I know. Jesus died on the cross and still now lives in me. He didn't just die for our sins. He died for everything that was bad on the earth. What I don't understand—why it is still happening."

I told her, "I don't totally understand that yet, either. But all I know it's probably because of people's beliefs."

She said, "My mother—Oh! I just realized this—She ran away!"

I said, "Where did she run away?"

"I don't know!"

I said, "But she will be safe."

She said, "She probably ran away from her job. It's too dangerous."

"What is her job?" I asked.

"It is to help people who fell in holes all over the world. But I don't know, it might have been because people were chasing her to get her money. She didn't go too far. It would be just another city. The woods were too far from there. There weren't many trees around."

I asked, "What city?"

"The next city—straight ahead." The girl thought she must have just gone to get something, because if she wanted to run away, she would go far. Even though she works all over the world, when she comes back for her money, she only gets a penny a day.

"Why is this country so poor?" I asked. "How do you buy food?"

"It's not supposed to be," she said. "It will change—to being rich."

Then I said, "You can't buy food. You just eat off of trees if you're poor. Or, hope that someone brings you food." I was thinking, "Why is this little girl so poor—when she believes." She should be rich." So I said, "So what was the miracle?—for your testimony?"

She said, "My mother found out there was food being given away—people taking it from place to place. And God gave her money. It's home safe. She hasn't used it yet. She wants more than enough, so she can give some away and still have enough for her family. She wants to spend it right, so she might be waiting to hear what God wants it spent on."

I said, "How is she getting much money?"

"She isn't getting much from her job. But she has $3 that she got from God, which is a lot of money in this country. It is locked up in a little box. She looks at it, and thinks how wonderful God is!"

I asked her, "What is the best job in this country?"

She said, "A job that gives you 50 cents a day. But it's not a job she was meant to do."

I said, "How is $3 a lot of money? How can you get enough food for the week?" There are no offerings, except what comes from another country. If you talked about offerings, she would say, "What's an offering?"

She asked, "Have you heard our legend?"

Most countries have bad legends. But this is a good one. It is something that gives a lot of money. Some call it a money ghost. But it's not God. But it's not as bad as some countries. I asked, "What did it come from—like what happened?"

"When this country first heard about God, they thought God is a person who gives money to people who deserve it. Then it turned people from a nice and wonderful God to a god that you have to earn. . so, isn't that better than some legends? A legend is usually partly true, partly not true, right?"

> The children and the mom know that God is good, and
> will give you what you need even if you don't deserve it.

The father believes the legend. Her mother told her that. "How did your country hear about God?" I asked.

"Some missionaries came. They told the people, 'God will give you what you need. He will give you money.' But, the people got it wrong."

In the end, I listened to her testimony. I was in the back outside in a group of chairs. They had a wood three-stairs stage. It was sort of a tiny cave, so it was out of the rain. They didn't have many buildings in their country. I heard from outside, people from other countries aren't allowed inside, unless they are invited.

They saw I was different, and knew I had come from Heaven. My skin was different. I was waiting outside with her until her turn. Their skin was a little darker, and the girls had really short hair. The boys had long hair. The girls and mothers didn't have as much money as the men. And, the mothers told the children to stay away from the men. The women and girls weren't meant to look as good as the boys. So they noticed my long hair, from another country. Not all had dark hair.

I was thinking about this dream, and that I would like to tell my testimony of healing my brain. But, they might not invite me, so somebody else could tell it for me. I would really like it to be told in that country somehow. Maybe God will tell them, or I can send it from Heaven.

They have never heard of freedom like our country. All the girls wear very short skirts. They can't wear pants. I think their skirts were short because they didn't have enough money to get long ones. I know they really want a dress. If you gave them a dress, they would be so-o-o happy!

They had some stores—clothes and food. But it was outside, on stairs, and some were trying to sell stuff by the cave, too. They also preach there once a week. I don't know what country it is, but I've heard of it before. This was the first time I was there. There weren't many trees and it was hot!

MARCH 7

I was in Heaven, and I saw many people climbing up a stairs. I didn't know where it led to. They said it led to a higher part of Heaven higher than the high, high places.

The angels do a little worship, a little music, angel missions down on the earth. I said, "When will they be doing the next mission? I like doing missions!"

"Today," they said. So I followed them. And when we got up there, more than 3 or 4 stairs—it's many stairs like climbing up a mountain—the mission wasn't starting.

The angels said, "We were going to do one, but we did it earlier." So they were waiting for another one. I stayed up there awhile talking with the angels, did a little worshipping.

Then the mission came, around Heaven lunch time, like 5 o'clock in our morning. The mission was people on the earth needed a little help. It was a bunch of children in one family. So, we went down there.

The angels found the kids that were lost and couldn't find their way back. The angels pointed the way. And when they got home, they had enough food for half of the town, and we gave the other half. So it worked out.

Mainly they gave fruits, and we gave all different stuff—vegetables and rice. Actually, the angels gave the most. We gave different things at each house, and they gave fruit.

So, when we were done, the angels gave something to each house to remember them. Most angels don't do that. Then the angels said to me, "You did a good job on your first angel mission."

I was given a little reward—a kid reward—a little necklace that had a little bag on it, to hold little things a kid would find. I don't have anything in it, but I will put something in, that the angels gave me when I first met them a long time ago. It was a key necklace to put Heaven keys on it. I forgot I had it in my pocket, so I never put any keys on it. If I put it in the bag, I will remember to do it.

We went back to the high, high, high place, and worshipped. Then Jesus came up there, which He doesn't do very often. He said to me, "Come up here." (to the stage where the angels sing).

The angels said, "Go up."

I did. Jesus handed me a ring. He said, "This is my first daughter to go down on an angel mission, who did it, not because she had to, but because she wanted to."

And, I enjoyed it. It wasn't my first mission, but my first angel mission. I've done missions—speaking at a Muslim Church, feeding children, healing, a lot of missions. I can't number them. But, I've helped a lot of children.

Rachel is not talking about natural earth ministry.

God once said, "If you want to do a lot of missions, just tell Me."

I said, "Yes, I do!" So, I have done a lot.

So, I spoke above the crowd of people (on the stage with Jesus). "I've done a lot of missions just because I wanted to. When you have Jesus in your heart, you have a feeling that you want to help people."

"It starts by just loving Jesus, because God is a good God. And believe. If you believe in the wrong way, God will change it. It matters what you believe. They say, 'I know. But in our country, it's very hard to become a believer. You have to hide when you give your life to God.'"

"I know that is a problem, but God is going to help you. You will be hidden when you are standing there. You can become a Christian, and not have to hide. God will hide you."

These were people from different countries, but with same problems. They were visiting, just like I was. I guess they wanted to do missions a lot. I said, "You can help me do my mission next time, any mission, not just angel missions."

> "When you have Jesus in your heart, you
> have a feeling that you want to help people."

MARCH 8

I was in Heaven, and I said to Jesus, "When is my next mission?"

Jesus said, "Whenever you decide you want to."

"Well, what do you mean?" I said. "I want to all the time!"

He said, "I'm talking about whenever you decide you want to do it with an angel. You usually start out with an angel to help you with your mission. You can choose one of your angels anytime.

Then I said, "I have trouble choosing because I like all my angels. Can you imagine that?" *(Said like, 'Can you understand?')*

The rest of the time we talked about missions.

MARCH 10

I was in Heaven, and I saw Jesus. We just kind of explored—played in Heaven's field. I don't remember what we talked about. We looked at pictures, and talked.

Jesus said, "All the children on the earth are going to experience Heaven before I come back"—which that's everybody! And I don't know how He's going to do that!

Then we went to the Love Room. Jesus was a few steps away. His love was touching me, but I felt like He was touching me. It was the waterfall. It felt so WOND-erful! Then I crawled up to Jesus, and started crying happy tears. . the first time in this part of Heaven. I touched His knees. because I felt His love.

I got up and hugged Him, and kissed Him. He hugged and kissed me back. Then we went to the castle, not the Throne Room, but the Love Castle. I went to my room, and tried on some dresses. I sat down on the bed, and really felt Jesus' love—more than usual.

Then Jesus said, "You'll feel my love more than usual, more and more."

Then He gave me a hug and kiss. Then He gave me a gift. I opened it and it was all the rest of the Heaven keys. I put them on my key necklace, and put it on. I have forgotten the names of them. The keys are for the doors of your heart. . to keep them unlocked, and unlock doors that are locked. You lock doors by accident sometimes. I don't know if I have any that are locked.

The only thing I remember saying, "What a wonderful day in Heaven!"

And He said, "Yes, it is wonderful!"

MARCH 11

I was in Heaven, and I saw Jesus standing there. He said to me, "Who are you looking for?"

I said, "I was just looking around, seeing where we are."

He said, "It's time to go to the River!"

We had planned that. Oh, it was so wonderful! Jesus said, "Slide down it!"

"Where does it lead?" It was scary 'cause you couldn't see that it led to anywhere. It looks like it's going straight, but it actually curves around and goes up.

He said, "It goes different places different times. So I don't know exactly." It turns different ways different days.

I went down it, and it turned up toward the Heaven roof. "Why is it taking me to the sky?!"

He said, "I don't know why it's taking you up there. I know there is the high, high places, and the high, high, high places."

It actually took me up, and swirled around to the high places. Then Jesus and me went to the outside Alone Room in that area. And we talked to each other. And I encouraged some people on the earth. I remember Jesus saying, "This is the most wonderful time I've had with you. And it will be like this for three whole days!"

And I said, "Me too!"

MARCH 22

I was in Heaven, and saw angels who were getting dressed up for an angel play. By the time they were ready, they came out and acted out the time when the waves were moving, and the disciples were afraid, and woke up Jesus. Then He calmed the water.

The end of the play Jesus came around from behind me and said, "Great job!"

They said, "We were planning to have more of an audience than you and her!"

"Yah! I don't know what's going on with your audience today!" Jesus said.

The angels said, "They all wanted to come, but maybe they thought it was later. But, we are going to do a different one later on today."

Then Jesus and I went to a place to sit and talk. We pretended to be writing to each other, but saying what we were writing. At the end I said, "You are the most wonderful GOD ever! And I love You!"

Jesus said, "You are amazing! And I love you. I AM inside you."

Then we helped the angels get the chairs set for the next play. And we watched with other people who came. It was of Jesus raised from the dead. One acted out Mary—the other Mary. Another was Jesus. Then Jesus came to Mary. Some disciples came. Then they skipped to the part where Jesus went to Heaven.

Then me and Jesus just walked around and explored Heaven. I don't remember the rooms and some I cannot name them or explain.

MARCH 23

I was in Heaven, and I saw a rainbow. Jesus was there with me. All I remember is that we talked, and looked at the rainbow.

MARCH 29

I was in Heaven. . by myself.   I didn't know where I was, or where anyone else was. . never was there before.

Then Jesus came over to me. He said, "Don't you see that you've been in this room before?" But I didn't reco-nise it. I must have been there when I was really little.

Then Jesus said, "This is called the Room of Jesus. There are all different things every time you come. The things that people speak happen here. If it happened in other rooms, it would end up crazy!"

I think people would end up chasing each other! That's what I've been told. "So what's this room used for?"

"For all different things—whatever you speak" He said.

I spoke, "Waterfalls, come to life." I don't know how many! The rest of it turned to grass. . and we ended up outside. The waterfalls all did different things. Some mixed together. Others did their own jobs. Joy and Love mixed together. They always do. You can't have joy without love.

The River of Life mixed with all the waterfalls. You wouldn't have waterfalls without it. They have the history of the River of Life. It started with being the river of Joy. Then waterfalls 'hit it' and it became the River of Life. It doesn't make sense, until you've been in Heaven a really long time.

The history of all of Heaven. . I don't know very much. I know the River of Life used to be on the earth.

Hopefully soon, when people start speaking only things that are good (I know it's really soon), Creation will go with what we speak. And, we will see the waterfalls with our natural eyes on the earth again.

You will see, later on, how pretty the River of Life is. When it hits the natural realm, it becomes rainbow colors. And, then the Heaven earth part of Heaven won't be there any more. I know that, as a fact.

I believe that in three days, (which is three months), a LOT more people will believe, especially in our country. Other countries will come later on. He helped us, and He will help every country to have freedom. With God's help we will keep our freedom, no matter what!

Then Jesus gave me this ring as a gift that I opened. It is a ring to speak. He said, "You are ready to speak it—to believe it."

He meant to speak things, and they happen. He only gives it when He knows it's planned. You can be ready in your mind--maybe not in your spirit. But when you have the ring on, it happens. It is a spirit tool. You never see it with your natural eyes. But it's always on.

Ever since the 5th, you have been in Heaven with me. But I don't know where you are—just exploring. It hasn't been that long yet. 'Cuz a day in Heaven is like a whole entire month. And, you have a few more days.

Wow! Lord, and Angels, Help me with my AWARENESS plan! I don't feel like it's working very good yet! Is it sort of like coming out of anesthesia? Just keep shaking me! I'm gonna' be fully awake soon.

In Heaven it isn't day by day in earth days. Things seem a certain way in Heaven, but they're not as they seem. When I first went to Heaven, I could never understand the days.

It's like twelve months is like twelve days in Heaven. Heaven has a tiny bit of time—it has a little bit of what's on earth—until everyone on earth gets to know about Jesus, which I kind of think is everyone.

Whenever that happens is when Heaven won't have 'Time', and earth won't either. That might be a long time from now. It's like blowing up a balloon that takes a month to blow up.

Jesus said to me, "Remember that I AM always with you. I won't be with you exploring Heaven for a few days. It will be people. I will always be with you. So, if you need to see Me, just come to the Alone Room. You won't be exploring with Me forever.

I understand that the Alone Room is in my spirit. But, we can go to the high part.

After journaling this dream visit, we read a wonderful vision from Victoria Boyson about Heaven invading earth! There continues to be revelation from Heaven through other sources, that dovetails with what Rachel shares.

> *"Joy and Love mixed together. They always do.*
> *You can't have joy without love."*

MARCH 30

I was in the low, low parts of Heaven, where the children are. It's not really in your spirit like the low part of Heaven. It's lower, like in your body or something. It's a play area, like what Annika saw. *(Rachel's little sister gets 'pictures' now and then, probably more often than we realize.)*

It was a maze. It was green. And, it ended where Jesus was sitting, ready to tell a story. I tried to go through the maze, but there are parts where I almost got trapped and didn't know which way to go. Somehow I circled down and came out.

Jesus said all the kids should come sit in His lap. He has a very big lap! So I did. He actually told the story of Me! The story He told didn't even happen yet. It was a future story. He told two stories. The first one was a history story of how I got to know Him.

He had like, sock puppets that looked like the people He was talking about, instead of pictures. It was crazy, but I think He forgot what day and year it was! We talked about this, and decided He didn't say all the facts that didn't matter to little children.

So He started—"There once was a little girl named Rachel. And she never had met Jesus." (He used His name instead of 'Me'.) "She was four or five. And one night she didn't give her heart the way lots of people do. It was in a spiritual way, not during the day with words and stuff." (I never told this—that I gave my heart to Jesus in a dream—without words. Then when I woke up, I realized what I had done).

"She was healing lots of people, and I walked up to her, and said, "Are you ready to give your heart to Me?". . and start seeing Heaven with your spiritual eyes, and hear knocks. . ?" (I didn't even know that happened in my first dream!) "Then, the next day she saw her heart together."

Some people say your heart is broken—a divided heart. But, it gets put back together when you give it to Jesus. It doesn't mean you're sad. Your heart wants to know Jesus, but you won't let it.

I remember that day waking up the first time with a Heaven song! I wouldn't remember it until I heard it again much later. People might only hear that song once, but I got to hear it twice. For children four or five —they don't remember, so they get to hear it again.

Then the second story was about the future—about on earth when I'm no longer a kid. It was just facts, more than a story.

Jesus said, "She saw beautiful things with her natural eyes, as she was awake on earth."

"How can I see with my natural eyes?" I asked Jesus, because in Heaven you can interrupt.

"Didn't you once say? 'Anything is possible on the earth!'" (Then it seemed like it was just older girls listening—like my age and a little older.) "Things can happen, even if you don't think they are going to. You started flying with the angels in beautiful colors."

"After this 'vision' you started talking to people about it and explaining the colors. And, only one person understood. You weren't in your house. You were walking around on the sidewalk, talking to people, and praying for people." (God just pointed to people that I should pray for.)

"After you did all this, you said to that person who understood, 'We'll talk more about this later—about Heaven.'" Other people heard me and wanted to listen. I believe by then, lots of people will want to hear.

Jesus said, "You won't be speaking in a church, but people where ever they are. You'll end up in somebody's car—invited for supper, and you don't even know them. But they want to hear."

People will—any way they can—get to where they can hear about Heaven. I do not want to do it in a church, but anywhere talking to anyone who wants to hear. And many people will want to hear.

The rule in Heaven about being careful who you tell will be different because so many people want to hear. You'll be all over the world, in the streets, everywhere. Once in a while—if I'm invited—I would speak in a church, but I don't want to be known as going everywhere speaking in churches.

I could see so-o-o many people's ears were open to hear, from one side of the country to the other—even in America. They did whatever they could do to listen. They called me 'Jesus Rachel'—a new nick-name. It was like when Jesus was on earth in Israel; everyone wanted to hear. It was very wonderful. They also called me 'Rachel Joy'. When people listen, you get more nick-names. Like the angels, they have so-o-o many nicknames!

It ended with just Jesus and me, and then I wanted to know more. So we went to the Future Room. That's where I saw going everywhere, and people asking if others had heard of me, and people hugging me. I was doing what Jesus did when He broke the bread in two pieces. . coming into people's homes when they were having communion.

I went to Israel. Somebody invited me to their house at Passover Day. I joined in with them. I saw the place where Jesus died and where people say He rose from the dead. It's what I've been asking—to see my future. And I actually saw it with my very own eyes.

I went to rooms of people who are going back to earth. We talked, and they told me about when they would be alive again on the earth. One was a father of two kids—which he needs to come back. I know he will. I asked, "Who is your wife?" It was a weird name. "Her name is Mary, and her son is Jesus, and the others, Believer and Daisy. (They were in a dream I had, remember?) "My name is Barabas. But, my name is changed because of what I do. You may call me Joseph." (People call him Joseph or other names.)

I was looking for Judy—that just died. She was in the third room. So I think she is supposed to come back. They will come back at different times. They have a choice to stay or come back. Some said, "I want to come back to see my wife, or my kids," or because they are not done with their purpose.

A happy, happy joy waterfall. The water is pink.

April 2013
Age Ten

APRIL 3

The Flower of Life—a picture I got during worship. It was like a big flower coming down like a waterfall. We drank out of the center of it.

Reminds me of a dream long ago—vividly real. I was gazing at a sky-full of huge colorful flowers, like clouds. When I awoke in awe, I remember my mind began to question purpose, value, and probability of such a thing, until it almost invalidated it in my heart. But, I never forgot. And, lately, my heart is being awakened to the realities of that other realm where we live, and move, and have our being!

APRIL 4

I woke up with a song:

> *The Flower of Life; It's for us to drink.*
> *It's in the low places;*
> *It's in the earth, For us to use.*
> *It's not really up high; But it looks like it.*
> *All things are possible.*
> *The flower does everything!*
> *Heaven is here; Jesus is here.*
> *He is in us, and also the Low Places of Heaven.*

APRIL 16

I was in Heaven, and I saw a beautiful rainbow. Then Jesus was standing right next to me, and asked me what was different about the rainbow. It only had nine colors. They usually have so many colors, you can't count them.

"Why does it only have nine colors?" I asked.

"Because when I rose from the dead, it was three days. The next three days I was with the disciples. Then the next three days, I went back to Heaven." So, it took the Son of God longer to get there.

? ? Timing—A mistake? Misunderstanding? Or mystery? Interesting, but probably not important to decide right now.

I asked, "Why did it take so long?"

He said, "I had so many things to do along the way. I was dropping Glory and Peace to a lot of people on the way back." He had so many stops to do—good stops.

"What happened the day you arrived?"

Jesus said, "All the people already in Heaven, not just from Israel, but in other countries—they were just living with their families. And I just took them there with Me. They didn't have to die first." The people hugged Him, and the angels came out and started to celebrate. Then, He said, "That's the day when I stomped! — and made everything in the other place disappear."

I don't know why the day changed. That was in March. Now they celebrate it in December, when we celebrate Christmas. I guess there was more time back then than there is now in Heaven? Who knows?

 A verse says, "I will stomp on the serpent and the lion " (Psalm 91) But, He was saying, "I stomped, so you don't have to!"

I really needed to hear that, because on the earth, I was starting to give up. . in my mind—never in my spirit. . like when I wake up in the mornings.

He said, "Don't you know? All of Heaven is not just mine. It's yours! Everybody owns Heaven." That means Him and people, not angels.

Every princess and queen gets different names at times. Jesus asked, "What do you want your name to be? Queen Diamond, or Queen Jesus?"

It was hard to choose, so I said, "You choose." I liked both so much! So, He picked Diamond.

He said, "Here is something. Don't open it yet—until I say it's time."

Others have gotten presents like that, but it was my first. "Why not now?" I asked.

"Because if you open it now, it won't do anything. So you should wait."

Then I asked, "When will it be time?"

"As soon as you learn lots of Heaven songs," He said.

I thought maybe it was a tiny flute, or maybe a ring, a singing ring. When you put it on, it sings.

Then there was a tea party. I actually dressed in a fancy outfit, and a Heaven kind of make-up on my face. It sparkles, and has a good smell—if you get it on your hand. Then that can make you fall down, or jump up and down! I didn't want to do that at the table.

I put on all the necklaces and rings I had been given—ten rings. And in Heaven it doesn't look funny. It's actually pretty cool. Also, a bracelet that when you pick it up, it's a key. The button on it opens the bracelet. You wear it for dress-up, but you carry it around at other times because it unlocks every door in your heart, that have been locked for years. It's called the Eye Key. But, it is put in the tummy to unlock anything. It's called the Key of All.

There is a switch on the locked doors that you can switch to using the Key of All, if you don't have the other keys (like the Eye Key, or the keys of Love and Joy). You have to use both Love and Joy at the same time, to unlock. The third slot is for the Key of All. I have both sets, and I wear my key necklace too.

Then I went to the party. The angels said, "Wow! You're dressed fancy!" (They normally wear dresses in Heaven. But for tea parties, they dress like we do, in pants and shirts. Maybe they dress like the people they are celebrating with.) Some angels don't have wings. I don't know why. They just disappear when they go.

We had fruit—like Heaven piece of chocolate. Pretty sweet! When we were done, Jesus told the angels to leave, and wanted me to stay. I guess He didn't want them to hear. He told me to come past the kitchen to a couple of chairs. The kitchen is just an oven for baking cakes, and a counter for cutting the fruit—a very tiny kitchen. . not like ours. . no sink. . hands don't get dirty. . no dish-washer.

> "He said, "Don't you know? All of Heaven is not just mine. It's yours! Everybody owns Heaven." That means Him and people--not angels."

A Heaven love party

Jesus said, "Show me your rings."

So, I took them off. . and my two bracelets. Then He said, "Look at the backs of them."

It said, 'Kristamaroma'. And when I said it, the rings changed! Like the rocks on some would go onto another. How did that happen?! There's no magic in Heaven. Inside there is a trade flower. But on the bracelets it didn't change. It just showed where my other bracelets were. He had taken them to add other stuff to them. . like song. Day after day, I have added song. Somehow they were in the tiny box that I wasn't supposed to open yet.

After I sang a song to Him, He said, "Why don't you go open the box."

When I did, it almost went crazy with songs I had forgotten—my songs I had gotten from God, going so fast! "Why are they so fast?"

Jesus said, "They are my songs, too. I made up all the songs in Heaven and I can speed them up!" (There was a slow button on it, so I could slow it down.) "Wear these during the day," He said, "and you will sing the whole day. And people will follow you. I am also called The Song of God." (People in Heaven call Him that.)

"When I first came down to earth, I had a lot of songs in my heart. When I got back to Heaven, I wrote them all down. And you wrote down what you've gotten, too. Tomorrow, I will show you the other History Room, histories of people living now on the earth. Are you ready? Meet me at the Love Tree!"

"I think we will always be a kid to God. "

"OK!" I said. Then, I got another gift—to wait till Christmas-time, when they celebrate the other feast (of His return to Heaven). That won't be long—only twelve days (one day is a month).

Then Jesus gave me a hug and I went back to my body with the angels. I only saw that once before—just by myself.

April 23

When I'm with Jesus, I always feel like a little child. With the angels, they see me as older. I think we will always be a kid to God. Some of the angels see me like Jesus does. Three of mine do. In your 'group' of angels, they are mixed—all different in how they hear. It's different how you speak to them in the low places or, in the high places. You have to be really LOUD in the high places.

Jesus had us in mind before He created the earth. He created the angels the day after He rested. On Sunday He created the angels. Only God knows when the baby angels were created. It seems like they were always there—like before the earth.

Some say they were created by accident! They know they didn't come out of the big angels' tummies. So they don't know. .

When God was lonely, He didn't have the Big angels—only some baby angels. They don't have a mom. They only have a daddy—God.

April 25

I told Rachel about my friend Connie who was crippled from childhood, in Borneo, where her parents were missionaries. She has been expecting to be healed for many years. We talked about the dream I had years ago—of her being totally healed. We talked about the dream I just had of her being partially healed, but not completely, about the disappointment of her missionary parents years ago that she didn't get a miracle. We talked about believing it is still going to happen.

I was talking about people I've seen in the History Room—people who are still living, people with that same kind of problem (polio). And maybe she was one of them.

I have been wondering why I am waiting to go down and heal them. Maybe they aren't ready. Mostly they need to be healed in their spirit, and then their body heals.

I can heal children easy because they believe. But adults don't have enough Heaven realm in their spirits. There is a natural realm in our spirits, and a Heaven realm. Some, like my mom, have very little natural realm left. That's very few. Lots of them don't believe at all—no Heaven realm.

When a daughter, or son experiences Heaven a lot, it really affects their family. Or if you are listening, and reading other people's experiences, it gets in your spirit.

You can see somebody's spirit, like through binoculars, how fast their spirit is getting filled with Heaven realm. You can have experiences of Heaven, but still not have it in your spirit—like how much stays.

I used to just have only natural earth realm. I didn't really believe in His love and stuff. And that's how it is with grown-ups. Their minds are just too attached to earth.

When you get so attached to God's Love, your spirit gets more of Heaven realm, and you can count the stars and so much more.

In a dream long ago, I saw two sisters that lived across from each other. One represented grown-up spirit—how slow they are to growing in God (wrong thinking). The other one represents your own spirit with Heaven realm. She was the younger sister. She represents kids.

April 28

I was in Heaven, and I was with the angel at the place where I go down, sort of through a Heaven telescope, that shows you what's happening down there. It's weird, because it's really tiny—the holes that you look through, and go through, a very small doorway and you're really BIG!

"Why am I doing it NOW?" I asked. I only saw a couple days ago, those grown-ups in a country, and how their lives were. Jesus never sent me down to help adults before. These I saw in the History Room.

They will build a History Room for kids, too. It's a fast way to build. Jesus, or the angels, just say, "Build!" and it happens! It doesn't work yet with people. I tried it once, pointing with my finger! But, it will happen soon. The angel said, "You have the answers. That's all you need."

"What? I had the answers a couple days ago?"

She didn't reply.

Then, I said, "Why aren't you talking to me?"

> *"Mostly they need to be healed in their spirit, and then their body heals."*

"I don't know why it didn't happen a couple days ago," she said.

Okay. First, I need to go get the people from my first angel mission to go with me. I promised them, because they wanted to go on missions. They lived in the high, high places. They won't be living on the earth much longer. They want to go. They have aunts there but they are supposed to come back. They don't want to, and they aren't in the right room yet. But they have a purpose, and they will want to sometime.

Actually they didn't die, so they won't be raised from the dead. They went up a ladder a few years ago (which is a long time ago). After Jesus went back to Heaven, many people lived a very long time. These people were from then. . and they don't look old. Even on earth, they look very young. Their family isn't sad about them leaving. I think they live mostly in Heaven realm.

So, I went to get them. They said, "Do you know where our aunts are? They wanted to do missions too." So, I ended up taking four people!

The angel was surprised! "How will we fit all four of you in the tiny telescope tunnel!"

I said, "There is another way—like a big glass window—but it's a door."

So, we all went through that way—angels like to take all together. It would take too long to shrink each one by one—to go through the tunnel.

You don't press the button by accident. It's only for missions, not for being curious. Then, if you go down, they'll have to bring you back.

We went to different places, even though we were meant to go together, holding hands. We all did the same things, but in different countries. We prayed for people, gave food, and healed the sick.

On the way back, we all ended up together. I took them back where they were. Then, I talked with the angel. She said, "You did good!"

"Where did we all go?" I asked.

So she showed me through the telescope where we all went. (It stays for awhile, so you can see.) I went to Africa. I always go to Africa! I went to Asia, and to the Philippines. Sometimes I go to South America. The last mission—I think it was in South America. I've been to lots of countries in Africa.

I went to see Jesus, and He asked how it went. He should have known! "It went great!" I said.

He said, "Are you waiting to see the part you've been waiting to have built?"

Yes!" I said. We went through some rooms. Then there was a door.

He said, "Build." And it was built! It took like three minutes!

I thanked Jesus. "And," He said, "We'll try it out right now." It showed kid's history and my history too.

> *"Jesus had us in mind before He created the earth."*

May 2013
Age Ten

MAY 1

I was on a mission. I didn't start from Heaven—like I usually come down the telescope. I was in South Africa. I passed by Gunter and Patricia's to say 'Hi', but couldn't stay long. I was on a mission to encourage grown-ups.

I said to some people—that I didn't know in earth realm, but in spirit realm only—"What is wrong?" It didn't look like anything was wrong.

The mother said, "I don't know. I don't think anything is wrong, but you were sent here to pray for blessing for the family."

I was quite surprised, because I usually pray for one thing that they need. Then I saw, kind of in a blink of my eye, an aunt of the girl (the two-year old who was in the wreck, and I raised from the dead). And the girl said to her aunt, "I saw Jesus—just two seconds ago!"

The aunt wanted a baby for a long time, and she had one a year ago! I just kept walking and praying for other people. Then I came back to her. She invited me for tea.

I said, "Maybe I can come in." But I was thinking I might have to leave soon to go back to Heaven.

She said, "When you do a mission, and you don't come from Heaven, you can stay longer."

"How do you know?"

"I've had others who have come," she said,"—not from Heaven. They just ended up here. Some have stayed the whole day. ." which would be like a month on warth. Heaven time is shorter than earth time. So a year down here is twelve days in Heaven.

So, I went in for tea. "I will stay with you for a day and a half," which is like a month and a week. It will be around the time we leave for Canada and Malta. So, I expect to be at her house for a while, in my dreams.

INTERLUDE WITH MAMA

Jesus said, "Didn't I tell you a minute of Heaven is like an hour?" There will be a time when there's no time. . anywhere. That might be a long time. It will be a time when everyone—I mean EVERYONE believes! By then, we will know everyone. Everyone will know everyone!

I already know everyone in Heaven-realm. When I'm on earth, I don't know everyone. It's hard to explain, because everybody lives in Heaven realm. They just don't know it.

"Can you tell a difference between the ones who have died and live in Heaven, and the ones still living on earth?"

"There are only two different skins of people in Heaven. The people who have died, and live there have darker skin. The ones who are still alive have lighter skin. Also, the people who have died don't show age. They say they don't have any age. The rest show the ages they are on earth."

155

MAY 11

I came from a country, back to Heaven, to a room of celebration. I don't know what kind of celebrations they have there. . different and probably not very often, or I would know about it.

I was just walking around, and wondering when I would go back down to that country. All of a sudden, Jesus and an angel 'popped out' right beside me! I was so surprised! "Why did you pop out and surprise me?"

Jesus said, "What? This has never happened to you before?"—like a person would say. He doesn't usually talk that way.

"What are we celebrating? I asked.

"It's YOU!"

"We haven't done that before," I said. Then, when they started celebrating, the angels and Jesus were circling me. I was in the middle dancing, and only my angels were dancing around. Nobody else came Soon Jesus started dancing with me. He kissed me and hugged me.

Then, the angels left. And right after that, I left to go back to that country. I went to the lady, where I was staying. It was kinda' funny, she said, "The day is almost over." No one ever said that before.

I said, "There's a couple more weeks."

And she said, "Two more weeks means the day is almost over."

We were sitting at the table talking. "So, what are we doing?" asked.

"Normally food just comes on the table, after you have been celebrated in Heaven," she said. "It's just not happened yet. It doesn't normally happen when you just arrived."

Then in three seconds it happened!—all kinds of Heaven fruit. She had poured tea, but said, "Don't drink it yet." I guess she wanted to wait, and have it with the food.

So we ate and drank. And then I played with her niece, the two-year-old (the one I raised from the dead). We played Heaven hide and seek. . up high hiding in the tree. I counted in Heaven numbers. There are Heaven colors and Heaven numbers, written like it sounds in some Heaven language.

Once I found her, we hopped around. I was partly in Heaven, so if we would run, our feet wouldn't stay on the ground. We couldn't race. We just played silly a little while.

I said an early good-by to them. They were wondering why. I had to tell them, "I'm just going to visit somebody—not leaving the country."

So, they followed me. They wanted to help me finish my mission. We each prayed for somebody different. Then the weirdest thing happened, that I had not done before. I was suddenly flying really high, like to the top of the world, above Canada—that place way up there—North Pool.

"Why am I here? No one lives here!"

The lady who flew with me said, "That's exactly why you're here! You need some time alone. . with me! People do live here, but they don't come out unless nobody is here."

We sat on the ground in the snow, with our feet on the edge of the ice. . where you could skate. But we weren't cold. In Heaven no place is cold. We talked about all the wonderful times she has had in Heaven, and with her niece. She has been baby-sitting for a year and spending time with God every day.

We talked about all the wonderful times in Heaven. That's what you talk about, and it just goes on and on. We talked about a few things, but we weren't staying that long. You would never get done!

I started to hear a tic toc, like a clock. "Why am I hearing a clock?" I asked.

"It's not a clock," she said. "It's your brain bringing back all your Heaven memories."

You don't see it happening, but it can go back to childhood memories. It's sort of like a clock without numbers, with a big arrow. The 'little hand' is on the inside. It's a Heaven clock, or you could call it a brain clock. Where the numbers would be, there are memories.

We talked about some memories. Then we flew back to her country, South Africa, and we baby-sat. The baby had gone back to her mother while her aunt took a little break. The baby said, "Won't you be leaving soon?"

"No, I have a few more weeks here." Then, we had tea and then went to the aunt's room, and sat on her bed to talk. She had three bedrooms. One was for guests, one was hers, and one for the little girl.

> *"What are we celebrating? I asked. "It's YOU!"*

The little girl said she has been staying there for a year, which isn't very long in Heaven time.

After we talked for a while, we all went to our rooms. I saw Jesus in all three rooms. So I talked to Him, "Where should I go?"

He said, "Come back with me." We went back to Heaven.

Then I woke up with a vision of us walking from one side of the world to the other side. . walking on water, for sure. We went from Africa back home to Florida, then South America. We kept walking and walking, around the world. It was a new experience for me to have a vision of that.

MAY 13

I was in South Africa, just wandering around town by myself. Everyone was in their houses, but not sleeping. I wandered where the people I was staying with. Then I saw Jesus, and asked Him where they were.

He said, "They're up ahead of you." He meant in the lower parts of Heaven, not in the country part of Heaven.

Then, since there were no people to minister to, and no mission to do, I just went to Heaven. *(That sounds like a one-liner that needs to be framed!)*

Jesus gave me a present, but told me not to open it.

"Why?" I asked.

"Because it only has one song, and you will get tired of it too soon. Come to the Believing Room," in the waterfall that is sort of hidden to those who don't believe. We went in the little doors to the rooms into the bigger room. We had to shrink a little to get through.

I heard music in the waterfall. Love songs:

> *Jesus made everything!*
> *Everything works by Love!*
> *Keep the thing working*
> *Keep the work (LOVE)*
> *Keep the work (LOVE)!*

The only reason Heaven works is because of His Love. The Love is most important of all.

Then Jesus gave me the most wonderful jewelry of all I have. It gives you the power to sing back to the words out of that waterfall. Its the bracelet of LOVE—which is also JOY. You can't have either one without the other. It doesn't work, unless they work together.

We went on to the Joy Waterfall. Jesus said, "Take away the bridge."

I said, "I don't know how to. . "

"Sure you do!" Jesus said. "Just keep on singing the song you were singing. Instead of singing, 'Keep the works. .' sing, 'Keep the Love and Joy' instead."

So I started singing that. The bridge just went to the side, and the waterfall was there!

He said, "When you slide down it, you will come to a tiny island—

Peace flowers

Heaven island—which is meant for songs, the Song Island. It's for songs of Love and Joy. It doesn't work when you're alone. We'll go together!"

We listened. And then we sang:

Love is wonderful; It is everything!
It won't work alone; Love and Joy work together.
The Love Key, The Joy Key, It only works together.
You won't have real Joy, Unless you have Love.
You need the two keys, To unlock the door.
Everybody is made with Love!

I have real Love. I am happy and laugh a lot. If you have fake Joy, it just lasts for a second. Real Joy lasts forever.

When the wind blows on the earth, it makes music in the trees in Heaven. Trees in Heaven are like trees on earth that kids like to climb —not too big. It tells me that maybe we had wind in the night while I was sleeping. Then the birds came. They landed on my arms. I started laughing when I saw birds all over Jesus—His head, His arms, and all the way down to His feet! I wouldn't like that many! He could hardly see!

They were little birds. The mom's and dad's were in the trees. They started singing:

Love works forever! Love birds singing a song.
Joy forever—Don't forget who you are!
You are the Love of God.
You are His Daughter!
The Holy Spirit in you!

The little birds tickle! The big birds not as much. Then the birds came off of us, and were flying around us as we were jumping around.

Then, we went back the Up-slide. Jesus said, "There is a lot of music in the gift, so open it now!" There were a lot of whistles. In Heaven whistles make song sounds. It sings with you. On earth I can't whistle. I put the instrument with my others. And I put my jewelry away, too.

Then we went back to South Africa, blew the whistles, and made music. We talked and had tea. Jesus was still there with us. We sat on the bed and talked. Even though every one knows what you did in that day, you still like to talk about it.

I gave Jesus a big hug. Then I wanted to take a nap. I never wanted to do that before. . in Heaven. I liked the rest.

While I was sleeping, resting, I was seeing Jesus. We were in a basket thing dropping peace flowers all over the world. We were singing all the songs, and Jesus sang my love song to me again.

MAY 17

I was at my house (in a Heaven/earth place), and I was talking to four men about sick people. And Elli was one of them. They told me they are not sick anymore. They are walking and talking!

Then when we got in the car, I was in the driver's seat. But I was not driving. You don't need to use the steering wheel. It started flying!

I noticed the mens' faces kind of went away. They didn't have eyes and mouth. They had hair, but not the parts that show what they're feeling. I've seen that before—that you can take off your face—even like a joke! It didn't seem weird.

The car was in a 'balloon-like light'—gold/yellow. When we got over the ocean, about three minutes away from where we were going, the 'balloon' sort of popped. We fell down into the water. We had to swim the rest of the way.

We came to an island, sand and trees, and three houses. The funny thing was there were too many people for the houses. They invited us to stay overnight, but we didn't know who it was. There weren't any hotels, just a few outdoor carts or stands, where they sold stuff.

When the people believed, another house would be built.

I flew back in the car, and the men swam back. When we got to my house, two of the men were talking about why this happened. One said, "That wasn't real!"

But, the other two said, "Of course it was real." They talked about why they fell. They decided it was because they stopped believing.

They apologized to me. I said, "You don't have to apologize to me. I'm just your guide. You can apologize to God."

But, they didn't see anyone else to apologize to. Then they went to their house. And I went to mine. I wasn't lonely because God was with me. I like being alone with Jesus. I think that represents a lot of people around their siblings or their wife, and it's hard to get 'alone time.'

> *"I learned not to give up what I'm believing. There are times*
> *I start to give up, but I get with God. I can be with Him all*
> *the time—even when people are around."*

Rachel Thoughts

I thought about the dream a lot. I learned not to give up what I'm believing. There are times I start to give up, but I get with God. I can be with Him all the time—even when people are around—even if you have seven sisters and brothers.

I was not on a mission. It was just an enjoyable trip. We explored around the island. I wondered why I fell down with the men because I believed. I always believe. *Mama: " But, in the end, you did fly back."*

May 29 -- Talking with Crystal

I was talking to her about being an angel mother. She said, "I need a little help figuring out what the pictures are gonna' be."

I was saying, "What about putting pictures of Jesus in there?"

The pictures that are in my second bedroom.

"What are you talking about?" When she understood, she said, "That seems right." They are pictures of Jesus with a flower in His Hand, and one of just His Face.

So we went to a long hallway of pictures—all of Jesus. It is for the angels to pick from. The pictures in my room were painted like painters see Jesus, not the way I see Him, the way He really is.

I was pointing to the one Akiane did, and Crystal thought that was the one. We chose it because we thought the baby would like a picture of the way Jesus really looks. It was BIG. It about filled the entire wall!

Akiane is the child artist that paints what she sees in the Heavenly realm, with precise accuracy. Amazing! BIG! And Beautiful! Rachel knows about her. Interesting that one of the little boys who recently went to Heaven also says Akiane's picture of Jesus is exactly what Jesus looks like.

We asked the angel that works there if we were allowed to take it. Some pictures have to stay there. Actually, he was one of my angel friends—about the only boy I know. This was the first time I met him. Usually, Jesus and Angel Mother choose your angel friends when you're a baby.

"The angels should have brought me to you sooner!"

I said to him. "You may take it, if you're not taking it to the high places."

"It would be too big," he said. The angel copier makes another one to hang in the hall. There was already another one of Akiane's—almost the same.

"Where are you going to put this picture?"

We were in the room, looking at the bigger wall. On the other wall, you could see more sky. Babies like to see the sky. I said, "There should be an angel picture on this other wall."

"No," said Chrystal, "I think we'll choose angel friends first." There were lots of angels there from the high places. So we have to try them out. . sometimes on the brothers and sisters. That's if the angel mother decides that. Sisters, when they're babies in Heaven, they like the same things. When they get big, they choose different things.

The angels were all on one little stage. They would have to speak, and the sister would say "Yes," or, "No." She said, "No" to most of them, "Yes" to only two which were from the low places.

I told Laughy she was a better mother than she thought. I was glad she chose for me. She was just an ordinary angel, so she thought any kind of angel could be a friend.

When the baby was able to speak normal with the angels from the low places, she couldn't understand the ones from the high places. I said, "Chrystal, you are doing a good job!"

She pulled out a picture of an angel with a rose in her hand. "Why?" I asked.

"Because her name is Rose." Then she put the picture up, and the room was done! The bed was ready. And Chrystal said, "I'm ready to born the baby."

For the first time ever I got to watch when the angel and Jesus borned a baby. Normally they want to do it secretly. Her tummy got a little bit big. Then it came out, and jumped into Jesus tummy. His didn't get big. He just pushed once, and the baby came straight out of His tummy.

Very interesting! And we know the spirit 'womb' is in the same place as the physical womb—definitely the area where we 'birth' spirit realities.

The angel mother grabbed the baby, and carried it to the bed. It was born sleeping. A lot of babies are totally awake. That's the way I was when I was born in Heaven.

> *"Its the bracelet of LOVE—which is also JOY. You can't have either one without the other. It doesn't work, unless they work together."*

Then—time to choose more angel friends. A whole line of angels from low places. She said, "Yes! Yes! Yes!" She said 'Yes' to all of them! They were all the kind the baby will like. She said, "My name is Chrystal. What are your names?"

The first said, "Chrystal Light". She looked a whole lot like Chrystal but different color hair. They were probably angel sisters. The next one was Rose.

The third one was Cookie. "People say I'm sweet as a cookie!" She said.

Then was Lady, a wonderful name. She was the first baby angel Jesus created, before the world. So, it means 'first'. She is a baby.

The last one was a boy. His name is "Gogetti". It's funny, simple and catchy. Maybe a nickname. . to go get things! I don't really know the meaning. He's a helper.

Then she showed them to their rooms, and put their names on their doors. Chrystal Light left her room kind of open—like her sister liked hers. Most angels have hidden rooms. Now Chrystal has a mother room but still open. It's a rule for angel mothers. Their rooms have to be in the open, so babies can always find them. So, Chrystal and Chrystal Light's rooms were so close, they were just a step away.

She went to check on the baby, and she was wide awake! Her first job was to bring the baby to Jesus. Sometimes it is taken to the mother angel's sister who is sort of the half mother. They look the same except for her hair, and they work together to care for the baby.

Laughy had an angel sister who may have helped when I was a baby but she is not well-known now. They had the baby in Chrystal Light's room, and taught her a couple Heaven facts. . a little song:

You were born out of me first,
And then into your Father. .

[That's what you have to learn first. It's normal that the Father borns babies. But, on earth, it's not normal. Jesus and God borned the first people ever. So Jesus has been borning kids for years! His Father did it before Jesus became a man.]

Since Rachel doesn't go to public school, her understanding of birthing is what she has heard and picked up at home. It is probably much more limited than most other American children.

After a little while. . You'll come in a person's tummy. And you'll come out. . into what we call earth.

That's what they teach. They have to know that their life won't only be in Heaven. They will have to go to earth. And they might not want to.

Then I wanted to hold the baby. Normal size in Heaven is very small.

Chrystal said, "No, it's not time for people to hold yet. At least not for six days (six months on earth)," which is almost the end of this year.

May 30

I was with Jesus, and I said, "Don't you think Heather's second baby is so cute?" I was talking about in a couple more years. "I haven't seen my baby room for a long, long time." So He took me there. I was so surprised! I saw the pictures of Jesus, and on the other side, Laughy. That's what you normally put—the pictures of your mother and father. And the Father is on the bigger wall, a bigger picture. (I mean Heaven father and mother).

The wall was pink, and I had dresses in there—a whole bunch—and in Heaven colors. "Laughy sure did a good job! Can you show me my old crib?"—'cuz now I have a bed in there.

Jesus said, "It's the same crib that is being used for Heather's second baby." They only need it for a day or so, because they will be walking then, and get a regular bed. And when the baby chooses their favorite colors, they change the room.

Jesus said, "Everything is good here right now. Let's go see the baby!" It was awake and crawling! And usually crawls to its' angel mother. But it crawled right over to me! which is not normal.

"Why is the baby coming to me?!"

Chrystal said, "It wants to climb up you, and can't climb all the way up me."

"But, you said I shouldn't hold it for six months." So, it wasn't normal, but Chrystal said it was fine for me to hold.

Then I saw her shelf—where there were angel names (of angel friends) in Heaven language, and earth language, leaving space for extra languages learned on earth. Also pictures of her angel friends. It's to help you if you forget. Chrystal made it. And when you learn another language, the picture comes off to make room for the other name. For a lot of people the pictures are still there, because they didn't learn another language.

I told Jesus, "I got to hold the baby before six months old!"

"That's why I brought you!" He said. Then He gave me a baby ring. And He gave one to the baby. That ring means, "You forever are like a little kid—a baby—to Me. If you get old in the natural realm, in Heaven you see yourself as little. This is how old you really are. This is how I see you."

When you're young on earth, He sees you as a baby. Then when you get older, He sees you as a child. Pretty soon people will realize that they don't have to look old at all. They will look exactly young. It also proves to you that what's on the inside of you will show on the outside—entirely. It's already happening—starting to happen—just 'DRIP'. .!!!!

Oh, yes! This is exciting for many of us who are expecting the re-newing of our youth! It's already begun!

MAY 31

I was in Heaven, and I only asked two questions. It's the shortest dream I ever had.

"What is going on today—with the baby?"

He said, "It's almost ready to walk."

"How come the baby knew how to climb before it knew how to walk?" I asked.

He said, "Some babies know how to crawl and climb before they walk."

I said, "That makes sense."

I decided to go back to South Africa. But when I did, they said they didn't need me anymore, so I should go back. So, I went back, and all I remember is, I rested. And the angels were going around me in circles. I don't know why.

Angel healing a baby

June 2013
Age Ten

JUNE

I was in Heaven and saw Chrystal again (this dream was less than an hour). I asked, "How many babies would you like born in this family?"

"Not anymore in this family. But maybe in Tami's family."

In case you are wondering, I was not asking questions or mentioning Heather or Tami. I usually only ask or comment at the end.

"That's unusual. No other angel mother has taken care of babies out of two different families. No one has thought of it before."

Then she said, "It will be a lot of extra work, but it will be worth it."

It's time for Jesus and angels to enjoy an angel mother having more than one. It will be a while before they choose the angel mother, because it will be after the first one gets in the earth tummy—the mother's tummy.

JUNE 2

I was in Israel, and it was time to walk around the wall—in history—the Jericho Wall. Six days, one time—and on the seventh day, I was a girl as a priest! I was blowing a horn. Is the wall going to fall on me?!!! It fell, but not on us!

To me it means: 1) It used to be that only priests went to the special box. But now we're all priests in a way—to experience Heaven. 2) Things are going to happen when I don't expect it at all. Walls falling down is example of surprises for good.

I'll take it as a sign of BREAKTHROUGH'S today! And, TODAY might be any day. Every day is eternity NOW!

> *"When you're young on earth, He sees you as a baby. Then when you get older, He sees you as a child. Pretty soon people will realize that they don't have to look old at all. They will look exactly young. It also proves to you that what's on the inside of you will show on the outside—entirely."*

JUNE 3

I was a little surprised that I started in South Africa. I walked around with the same people, around town. They said, "Come with us."

We went to a beach, but I don't know if it was a beach or a pond. We didn't sit on the sand, but we did swim a little. I said, "Thank you for bringing me here."

After that, we said to two more people who were with us, "Are you going to our house?"

"Yes," they said. "We were invited to stay over."

None of us knew them, but somebody had invited them. (On earth) one of the children had called on accident. But it was OK. I asked all of them the same question: "How did this happen?"

"It happened on accident!" Then they came to the house, which wasn't very big. But they said it was the biggest one they had seen in

South Africa. They looked like. . um. . two men with red hair. They were tan, but I don't remember what color—brown or black? They looked way different than my friends. They were born in a different country.

When we got back to the house, I asked, "When did you decide to come to this country?" We were thinking and didn't know when they got called by accident. "Where were you before you came here?" I asked.

"We were actually in part of the Philippines."

"Why were you there?" I asked.

"We explore other places more than we stay at home. We stay home for a day (which is a month on earth). Then we leave." They enjoy travel. It wasn't a mission.

"Where do you live?" I asked.

"We live—we'd rather not tell where." So, they didn't tell me. But the people I was staying with knew. But they kept it a secret, too.

So I said to them, "Why do you like traveling so much?"

"Staying at home is boring. There's no place to explore. It took a couple years to explore the entire country."

They ate with us, and slept with us.

> "It used to be that only priests went to the special box.
> But now we're all priests in a way—to experience Heaven.."

JUNE 4

I was talking with Jesus, walking in His tree garden. The trees grow automatically, but He said, "I started it, so I call it Mine!"

I asked, "Why is this place so quiet?"

"Not many people know about this."

When I was in the Love Tree one time before, it was in this garden. He keeps His fruit in this garden. When we walk there, I pick one fruit from one tree.

So, we just walked and talked, and Jesus said, "You're welcome to pick."

It's sort of dark there—shady, like when on earth we walk in the evening. He likes it that way.

JUNE 5

We were still walking and talking.

JUNE 6

I was still with Jesus in the garden. I asked, "How many people know about this place?"

He said, "You and Me and your best friend in Heaven" (a little kid, a boy). Jesus is my Best Friend.

"When did you start this place?"

Jesus said, "I knew that people would need to use stuff for their spirit for the whole entire year. And there was grass here. So I spoke trees to grow." (They grew in two seconds!) "I created this place before I created the baby angels. Then I created the earth and you."

When Jesus made the day and night, it says He called the light—Day. But, really, He called it Ma-huma. And, the night Ma-suma, or properly, Suma. This was Heaven language. The first language spoken on earth was Heaven language.

"Can we have a picnic here tomorrow?"

He said, "Yes."

I asked, "How many people see this place from the back and don't know what it is?"

"Pretty much everyone." He said a number that there isn't such a number! I didn't understand. But they just look in, and don't come in.

Then, I went to sit on my bed.

JUNE 7

We were doing a picnic. It was a 'pick your own' picnic off the trees. And we had a blanket. We picked a lot of kinds and a lot of the same kinds. I ate my favorites. I asked, "How many trees are there?"

He said, "More than you can count."

JUNE 8

Walking in the trees. I asked Jesus, "Do you have anything to give me?"

He said, "Yes, I do."

He never gave me a Heaven earring before. This was the first one—a set—The Diamond Love. It was called that because it sparkled like a diamond and diamond means love. Some people call it Diamond Diamond.

JUNE 9 (AT AUNT JUNE'S)

It was just me and Chrystal. "Do you enjoy being an Angel Mother?"

"I do enjoy it very much." I knew she would end up enjoying it. But she wasn't so sure about it at first.

She went to teach the baby another lesson. I don't know what it was. The baby was on the floor between us. The baby could walk now.

This is an interesting portrayal of how angels serve people—in this case, a baby, and a 10-year-old. And, maybe some don't know more about humans than a 10-year-old?

"Jesus went somewhere. He was still there.
I just couldn't see Him anymore. "

JUNE 10

I was alone at a waterfall. There was rock behind it, like a cave. I said to myself, "Where am I? I've never been here before!"

Then Jesus came, and said, "It's the Not-Known Waterfall. It's a secret place."

I asked, "Why don't You tell people about it?"

"Because they don't think there is such a waterfall. I can't even tell you about it. It goes along with history."

Some people call it The History Waterfall, because the name goes along with history. I was thinking that in all history, all bad things happening, but the whole point is—"I Love You." So, I call it The Love Waterfall. Then, I thought of the Diamond!

"Yes, that's it!" Jesus said.

I asked, "Does it have diamonds in it?"

Jesus said, "No. But do you know what diamond means?"

"It means Love!" I said. So, some people call it Diamond History Waterfall.

Then Jesus showed me around. We walked, and He showed me behind the waterfall. It was like a cave. It had pictures from Adam and Eve all the way to when Jesus rose from the dead.

What does all this mean? Diamonds. . it said, Diamonds. It means

Love.

Then, He took me out, and I just looked at the waterfall. Jesus went somewhere. He was still there. I just couldn't see Him anymore.

Profound!

The Diamond Waterfall is a copy of Living . The pictures are different, but it works the same way. Without Love you wouldn't Live. They both show love, but they show different things. One doesn't have pictures.

It really affected me. It was wonderful. I felt Love. But I couldn't see Jesus' body anymore.

These waterfalls—apparently sourced from the River of Life, but in specifically different Life-flows of inspiration, information, transformation life. Makes me want to visit them often.

> *"Jesus said, "You're asking the same questions people ask about Heaven— 'When will it change to be more than where we live everyday?" Jesus tried to explain—"The earth is Heaven, and Heaven is earth."*

JUNE 11

I was in Heaven and saw the place of The Little Waterfall and grass and a spark-like rainbow sound that went around and down. Then I saw a whole bunch of the same thing. They attached to each other in the sky in sort of a circle.

What appeared after it, was a rainbow of Heaven colors. . Like it was scattered, and all came together.

Jesus said, "Did you see how that happened?" He pointed to me, and said, "You are my rainbow. When you learn more of my Love, and about Heaven—then it starts attaching. I see your future as you're already a rainbow."

"What does that mean?"

"What does what mean?!" He said.

"When you said, 'You are my rainbow.'"

Then He said, "Do you remember that colors mean something? Every color is inside of you."

"Can I see it inside of me?" (I already saw it in the sky).

"Maybe. But just come with Me." We went to a place where there was a bunch of mirrors. Funny, but they were magnifying glasses. Jesus grabbed a magnifying glass, and put it to my tummy. And, I could see sparks. But, I didn't know what the colors mean.

Jesus said, "This one means LOVE. This one means JOY. This one means PEACE. And this one means FORGIVENESS." When there's sparks it's all the same color. But they all become different colors. Jesus knows what they become.

He said, "That's who you are. You have Love for everybody. You have Joy for everybody. You have Peace for everyone who needs it! It's starting to attach inside."

He took me to this room that had a whole bunch of different stuff in the sky. I can't name what they were. There were two chairs. Jesus and I sat and watched the sky. As I watched, I was learning more of His Love, more of His Joy, more of His Peace, and more of His Forgiveness.

Jesus said, "Let's pick up the magnifying glass again." When He put it the same place again (on my tummy), the rainbow was attached—it was put together.

After the Dream

I thought of the rainbow, that it's a picture of the way Jesus sees us. He sees that we have Love and Forgiveness. When people think they aren't very forgiving, Jesus says, "You are very forgiving. That's who you are!"

Oh, if everybody could just hear that!—a glimpse of who we really are!

And He has a rainbow in His Hand to show you what you are. Or sometimes He shows Love or Joy or whatever. . He shows the meaning. It depends on how the people are. He might speak it in reading. . in many different ways.

I never thought of rainbows that way before. They are a promise, and we will see what He sees.

Don't you often wonder about the beautiful sign in the sky, that it must have significance, something more than just no more Big Flood? Rainbows around the Throne. . Rainbows in His Hand. . Next rainbow, I will look 'beyond' the colors.

June 12

I was in Heaven and I was asking Jesus questions in different languages, and I didn't exactly know what I was saying. I said, "Are You able to translate this?" I knew He was.

Then He answered me in a different language, the language I speak. The question must have been, "When will the world change, or come?"

Jesus said, "Don't you know, the world is changing every day, little by little?"

"But when will it change completely?"

Jesus said, "You're asking the same questions people ask about Heaven. When will it change to be more than where we live everyday?" Jesus tried to explain—"The earth is Heaven, and Heaven is earth." *(Jesus is in me, and I'm in Him.)*

"When you hear the trees singing on earth—not just the wind—that's when I will be coming."

I hear the trees making music in Heaven, not words. but music like one instrument. I haven't heard the flowers or anything else yet. Angels sing sort of like people. And I also hear people singing, and playing instruments.

When He comes, He will just make us realize where we live. Because we already all live in Heaven. People think when Jesus comes, He will take us all to Heaven. But, really, all He will do is give us the realization that we already are in Heaven.

Jesus said, "The earth won't go away. The earth will be or act like, Heaven. You're going to stay on earth forever."

I said, "I knew that. . kinda'."

Jesus said, "Why were you talking to me in different languages?"

My answer was, "Cuz I just wanted to see what your answers were and kinda' guess what I said!"

After the questions, we just looked at each other, and didn't say anything.

I always thought when we go to Heaven, the earth will disappear. But Jesus said the earth won't ever disappear. It will just be different than it is now. Why did I ask those questions? I already knew the answers.

I don't know where we were. I just know we were in light. . light all around us. People say the middle of Heaven is white. So maybe that's where we were.

I guess all of creation has been groaning for a long time. How much are we tuned in to the sounds of creation? When we find ourselves straining, we have to learn to flip the channel. It doesn't work to just try turning down the volume of earth realm.

David learned that quite well—probably from early childhood—listening to the sheep, to nature, to Heaven, while normal kids went to public school. Then as an adult, his Psalms give lots of examples of 'flipping channels' from earth-realm to Heaven-realm.

I am 'tuning in' more often—especially since hearing Jesus' words to Rachel. It sounds so simple. But, I must have lost the 'remote' when I was a child! And, whenever I happened to find it, I couldn't figure out the buttons. Every now and then, I would happen to hit the right ones, and—WOW! WONDERFUL! Eventually, the brain comes up with formulas that seem to work once in a while. But, it's a long shot from living 'tuned in!'

I'm excited about the Heavens opening—with limitless possibilities for us all. "He that has an ear to hear, let him hear!" Tune in! Hear His Voice! . .the music! . .the waterfall! Listen to the trees!

JUNE 13 – 14

I was in the middle of Heaven alone. I started looking for Jesus where He likes to be in His trees. And He was there on a blanket, waiting for me. . like for a picnic.

All of a sudden, there were instrument angels behind us, circling us. They were all playing recorders, like flutes, but didn't sound like our recorder. They play to make things happen. They do it all around Heaven every day. They don't sing well. They're made to play instruments.

There's four in a group, and there were twenty-four. They played in groups one after another. Some of them sing and play at the same time. It's not easy for them, because their instrument is too loud. They say, "We can't sing very well, because no one can hear us!"

Me and Jesus were eating and looking at each other. Then He gave me a little gift. It was a tiny instrument. It looks like a recorder, but not.

"What is that for? It's so tiny!"

Jesus said, "Blow in it." When I did, it made a whole bunch of instrument sounds! *(Is all creation waiting for us to blow our instrument?!)*

Jesus said (in Heaven language what we would say on earth), "It's an instrument recorder."

As I was playing it, the sky was changing colors. "Why?"

Jesus said, "That's the way the sky sings! You can hear all nature singing with a 'hear-a-scope.' It makes your ears hear the quiet sounds. The trees, the flowers, the grass. . are the instruments. The sky is the

185

Voice.

I said, "I want to be able to hear without the thing."

He said, "It won't work down here. We have to go up to the high places."

We went up, and there was a new room there. In that room I could hear all the instruments of the flowers and trees. And the sky was singing. It's the highest part. Sometimes the birds sing with the trees too.

When I woke up, I was thinking about the sky, and how it's the highest place. You go to the high, high places, and then the high, high, high places and then you're just in the sky after that.

So then I had a vision. I was singing and all of a sudden I was on a spring that just shooted me up in the sky and I was floating. You could see like out an airplane window. Things look very small—of the lower Heaven—the high parts—all of Heaven—places you have never been.

I could see stuff happening. I could see a Light. It was the Father talking. It was higher than Heaven, a place where Jesus goes—only Him. It's hard to get there.

But there are people there—from back in the Bible. They went in through the Father. Not people from Old Testament—they are in the Low Places. Some people after the New Testament, too. It's like their bedroom. When you look in, you can just see books. It was the first room ever created of Heaven.

I've heard from other kids there are old, old stairs and sort of like a door from the high, high, high, places. The door is at the bottom of the stairs. I've never gotten past the door. There's so much glory, you just fall down. There's no door handle. It just pushes open.

JUNE 14

I was in Heaven, and I said to Jesus, "Would You take me to the highest room? I've seen it, but I want to see inside."

"Of course!" He said, "We'll take the back way, the way the children go." Everyone is a child, but He meant the little children. So we went, and He took me inside. I saw mainly beds and books.

"What are the books?" I asked.

He said, "They're future books. They will be made on earth later."

I looked in one book. It had a picture of me on every page—the same picture with words under it. I said, "We're going to make my dream book different than that."

He said, "We can't make it exactly the way you do it on earth. We make it here so that little children can read it." They somehow can read it, looking at the pictures.

> Mama says, "Yes, and maybe in Heaven realm, they see you on every page. I hope I will see you and Jesus on every page. Or maybe I will see myself with Jesus. We want to see what you see."

I put the book away. Then I asked, "Where are Mary and the disciples and the others that stay here?"

"They are in the History Room right now. They go back and forth—often using the back way. It's fast like a suction." People have to see the New Testament first, before they understand the Old Testament. So these people are in the History Room whenever people visit the New Testament part of the room.

I stayed for a while. I saw the vacuum thing. Jesus said, "You shouldn't go down it."

I asked, "Why not? I'm in Christ the Hope of Glory."

Jesus said, "Everyone is! Only the people that belong in the New Testament go down there" (to the Low Places).

"So what happens if I do?"

"It knows that you don't belong down there, and will bring you back up." (It's like a slide with a top to it.) "You can go down, but it will bring you back up!" Jesus said.

So I did go down. And back up. It was bumpy coming back up, and it was long and fast. Then the vacuum part went away. It wasn't needed anymore, so it wasn't there anymore. There was just a hole in the wall.

Jesus said, "It's also used to jump down to the ground." I wanted to try that too. I wasn't scared, but it was pretty far down. I made it—like a fast jump! I was right next to the History Room. I saw where the slide ended. So then I decided to go up the stairs. When I got to the door, it was already open! It didn't knock me down!

I saw the stairs. They did look very old. But I made it up. And the door at the top was also open. I went back in. Mary and the disciples were done, and coming back up.

Then they took me to this place where there was a desk and drawers. I have never been taken someplace with New Testament people! They opened a drawer and took out a picture of people in New Testament that people don't know about.

The next picture was what the people look like now in Heaven. On earth, they lived in the last book of the Old Testament, and lived in the New Testament. They were pretty old. Their hair was very grey. Now their hair was sort of yellow—like gold. They were more like twenty.

They had things that they had on earth—in a place to keep them safe. The things were a smaller version of the real. It was just to keep them safe—even though they don't use them.

The next drawer gets pretty interesting. When they opened it, it was glowing. They took out a picture of Jesus, and it was glowing! "Why is it glowing?" I asked.

The disciples said, "It doesn't always. Just when you see it for the first time." Under it was one of Jesus' keys, and some other things. I don't know what they were.

The last drawer, the third drawer—a whole bunch of things, and glowing too. Pictures of young people that live here now—tons of those. Under the pictures—facts, really good facts—about their lives so far.

Then Mary comes, and opens the second drawer. The picture of Jesus was when He was a baby. She gave it to me, and replaced it with the same picture that was there before—how He looks now. (When Mary opens the drawer, the picture changes to her Baby. When anyone else opens it, Jesus looks like He does now). So I took it and put it in my jewelry box. Mostly people don't look in a jewelry box for pictures, so that is where I put it!

Then Jesus came and asked me how I liked it there. I said, "It was wonderful!!!"

He knew that, but He wanted to hear me say it in my own words. He likes to hear how much we enjoy—even if He already knows.

I commented to Rachel, "That's a B-I-I-G statement, and we need to be reminded—often!"

WHEN I WOKE UP

I never thought of facts about people that are living now days. I've thought about facts of people in the Bible. I've thought about problems. But not about the great life people are living.

And, I thought about the trap—which was actually a cage, in the first drawer. I never thought about that before. They built the cage on earth to keep them safe. It was a trap to catch bad people—like Romans. Someone stayed up all night—like a guard. So this small cage had special small size things in it—like memories of their history for others to see.

When I realized this was the last entry before Rachel went to Malta for the summer, I smiled at how this book ended.. New Heights.. Treasures from History .. Mystery.. the sense that exploring Heaven never ends. It's only beginning for ALL of us!

.. to be continued!

Forever!

Epilogue

Now it is a year later, and we must not wait any longer to share this treasure. Though the dreams continue—more sporatically—and, 'day-time' awareness of Heavenly places increases, this first publishing of Rachel's journals ended with June 2013.

He said, "They're future books. They will be made on earth later."

I looked in one book. It had a picture of me on every page—the same picture with words under it. I said, "We're going to make my dream book different than that."

He said, "We can't make it exactly the way you do it on earth. We make it here so that little children can read it." They somehow can read it, looking at the pictures.

This was taken from the last dream recorded in this journal. How appropriate to end here, with Jesus talking about Rachel's future books!

As this first book goes to print, we are beginning to see more and more into that other realm we call Heaven—our primary and permanent residence. And in sharing Rachel's journeys, we are finding many others who have been exploring this wonderful new world—created just for us!

What could be more awesome, more breath-taking than wandering through 'Utopia' with your Best Friend, anytime you want?!! In a perfect world that never ends. Ha!

We are privileged to share what we have received. Our quest is to become *aware awakened* to the heaven realm—where we already are 'seated with Him'. And that we will begin to know our way around Heaven like Rachel does!

This is for the world to know. Our mandate is to make it available for the world—in many languages. And our hope is that you too, will enter through the door that Rachel has   found.

Dreams and Visions

I sometimes wonder, "Why do we need dreams?" Dreams are for learning about Heaven. But, why couldn't we just learn about Heaven during the day?

. . At night, my mind and body is so open to Heaven, while I'm getting ready for bed. But, in the morning and during the day, my mind is open to the earth. Why don't I think of Heaven all the time?—"Why does that happen?" I asked.

Jesus said, "Because your mind is very curious about earth when you wake up in the morning. . and throughout the day."

When Rachel was very young, we began asking her often if she had dreamed. We talked to her about lying quietly when she was just waking up—to 'connect' with what was in her heart mind. Sometimes it might be a dream, a song, a picture, some words.

Later, as her dreams increased, she told me she does what we had told her to do. And now she knows the difference, a big difference, between Heaven dreams and earth dreams that she calls 'silly dreams.'

It is so wonderful to hear that she understands now why she heard voices and was afraid at night when she was very small. And now she knows what is true and what is false. And that she doesn't need to fear what is 'fake'.

Both she and her sister see 'pictures' from the Heaven realm—usually more quickly and more often than we adults do. Revelations from the little people are profoundly simple, and mostly untainted by human mindsets. We have learned to ask them what they see, and then listen. And with asking, they are sharing more.

God has given the little people to help us big people. I have been inspired by Rachel to listen more. . to connect with the children around me. . to encourage their sensitivity to the Heaven realm. It is a sensitivity that children are born with. But, it fades away so quickly when they enter the earth realm.

Sadly, most parents are oblivious and race to see how much earth knowledge they can stuff into them, with competition, and incentive to be at the top of their class, etc., etc.

So children soon learn from adults what adults think is most important to know. Then, with the help of electronics entertainment, the daily schedule is filled and children's hearts become dull to the Heaven realm, just like their parents.

The good news is, there is a great awakening happening all over the earth! And, earth is tuning in to Heaven. . to a Father who deeply loves, and is communicating with His people everywhere.

Heaven is whispering to earth. If you want to hear, you will listen. You will hear. You will dream. And you will discover, Heaven is here now.

Rachel's Heaven treasure box from Jesus

From Some of Rachel's Special People

'DAD' DANNY ORSER

If you know Rachel, you know that she isn't given too much to fantasy. Her "make believe" doesn't take anyone too far!

Recently when she had a writing assignment, her mom said, "Why don't you write about one of your dreams?"

Her answer was, "No. That's real! I want to write about something I made up, that I imagined."

That is what makes the accounts of her dreams seem so very plausible to me. She recognizes a great gulf between make-believe and reality. Her quantum leaps to Heaven are engaging to young and old alike.

At first, I wasn't sure about what I was hearing. My old-school Pentecostal background didn't always jive with what she was telling. I would say to her mother, "I'm not sure if I agree with that.."

However, I couldn't deny that it was, after all, Rachel. . the literal one. The one who wouldn't—or couldn't lie even to her own peril. ("Did you break that glass, Rachel?—Yes.."). Her stories had to be exactly what she was really seeing. When a little child keeps seeing the same setting in dream form night after night, year after year, you begin to believe.

She's changed my theology quite a bit in the last couple of years. As I go back into the Bible and what I now believe about the Father's heart for people of every background, I see the pictures of Rachel's vivid visits.

There will be the skeptics, the unbelievers and even the haters of this book. The only thing I can tell you, as Rachel's father, is that there is no agenda here. No aspirations of an eleven year old to hit the book tour. Everything is pretty much word for word in dictation form as told to her Gramma.

The motive is pure. Keep an open heart.

'Papa' Lou Goszleth

In God's sovereignty, He chooses to reveal Himself to each of us in His own way. Our granddaughter, Rachel, has had visits to heaven on a regular basis.

Her simple, matter-of-fact scenarios have impacted and inspired me. One of my favorites is her visit to the Ball Room.

. . Then we walked to the Heavenly Ballroom! Once I got up to Jesus, I said, "I know You are here. . but what is this room for?"

He said, "When I come to get all of you, I will bring you to this room and marry you!"

Ever since I was in Heaven, I have wondered where that would be. It was so amazing, I fell down! That's what you do in Heaven when you are amazed and excited!

It is the most beautiful room I have seen in Heaven. . the walls. . the glory. . and no chairs, because nobody sits and watches!

Jesus said, "The angels will be standing all around the edges. And, you will know everybody's angels."

This is the first time He has told me anything about the future—in Heaven. The truth is, He doesn't even know when it will be. His Father knows, and He will tell Him.

I did ask Him, and I was surprised He didn't know. He said, "My Father even has surprises for Me! And for His little children."

We all know He's going to come back, but He doesn't know when.

Listening to her description of what she experiences has been revealing, enlightening, encouraging, confusing, etc. This book is not meant to be a doctrinal thesis nor should it be judged as such. It comes from a child who doesn't know what doctrine is, but knows what she sees and hears in Heavenly places.

You will get a glimpse of Heavenly realities through the eyes and understanding of a child. May faith and hunger increase for all that the King has made available for us NOW, and for eternity.

TRACY VANDERBUSH

In 2010, I had an incredible vision of a large, wooden bookshelf that was filled with thousands of books for and by children. From the books, waterfalls were flowing down the shelves and forming rivers that were reaching in many directions. Being that I was not used to having visions, I immediately asked God what I was seeing.

I felt the Holy Spirit speak to me, "I am pouring out my Spirit upon many writers and anointing their stories with healing that will reach into childrens' hearts. They will see visions and write of their encounters with Me. Hearts will be mended."

Little did I know in that moment when I spoke what I had seen, that there was a sweet mother in the audience that I would meet that day. And her amazing little girl, Rachel, is the one whose stories you hold in your hands. It has been my honor and deep pleasure to know the Orser family. If any family is absolutely dedicated to living in the presence of God on a daily basis and listening to the voice of the Father, it is them.

I believe that this book is one of those "waterfalls." It will not only bring healing to children, but to every adult who reads it, because all of us really are children.

BILL VANDERBUSH

From the audible voice of God bypassing Eli to get to the open ear of Samuel, to anointing the youngest of Jesse's many sons as king of Israel, to the borrowing of the womb of Mary for the unbelievably scandalous incarnation, God has always used the young to wake us up!, to challenge our theology, and to reignite the wonder of dreams.

I believe we all too quickly dismiss the words of a child by attributing fanciful thoughts to an overactive imagination. As if an underactive imagination is somehow a virtue or mark of maturity! Rather, it is that child-like sense of wonder —of limitless possibility—of unjaded perspective at the goodness of being and living. It is that child-like unstoppable faith! And it's not an option either. It's an absolute prerequisite to experiencing the Kingdom of God.

In the New Testament we are encouraged to leave behind that which is childish, while embracing that which is child-like. To be childish is to do life— blinded to wisdom and understanding and with no desire to gain either one. This is done by people of all ages and is the foundation of a religious mindset.

To be childlike could be defined as the ability to combine wisdom and understanding (that comes from education) with the limitless possibilities of the sanctified imagination.

Rachel's thoughts, dreams, musings, prayers, and contemplations in this book will absolutely challenge your childishness. Her dreams have left me stupefied realizing that without even knowing it, I had left some valuable childlikeness behind.

You may well find some things in this book that could be challenged by Scripture. And no matter the age of the thinker, nobody's thoughts are above the ability to be questioned. And, that is as it should be.

But consider this. God has made a historical habit of challenging our understanding of the Scriptures with a revelation of His goodness. So much so that when the teachers of the law—who knew the Word of God by heart—had God standing before them in the flesh, in love and grace, they couldn't recognize Him. For it's one thing to know the Word BY heart, and entirely another to know the Word IN heart.

To know by heart takes time and study, but to know in heart belongs to everyone with ears to hear and a heart to know His love.

Rachel Orser knows Him in heart, and perhaps seeing through her eyes, you will too.

DIANE CONNIS

I've known Rachel since she was born and her family long before that, so I can attest to the validity of Rachel's adventures in Heaven. Rachel is a very literal thinker and not a child prone to imaginations, but her divine encounters, full of joy, beauty, simple love and trust, are an unveiling of the wondrous heart of God for all His children, who sparkle like diamonds on earth when Rachel and Jesus view us from Heaven.

The most wonderful revelation in Rachel's dreams is this: Heaven is already on earth but we spend so much time mired in our natural and physical, temporary realities, we are often unaware of it.

We don't understand what being, "Seated in Heavenly places" (Ephesians 2:6) really means or what, "Christ in you the hope of glory" (Colossians 1:27) can do for us, nor do we totally grasp the concept of, "On earth as it is in Heaven" (Matthew 6:10). We don't realize that we are already living in eternity and this life is just a chapter in our own never ending adventure.

For those who read Rachel's journal with skepticism and doubt I would say, as God did to Job in chapter thirty eight and verse four, "Were you there when I made the world? If you know so much, tell me about it."

I Corinthians 13:9,10 and 12 tells me, "For we know in part..but when that which is perfect is come, then that which is in part shall be done away. For now we see through a glass, darkly; but then face to face: now I know in part; but then shall I know even as also I am known."

Who am I to think I know exactly what goes on in Heaven? We all have ideas, speculation, theological interpretations but how can we really know when we are looking through earth fogged glasses? I do a tremendous disservice to myself and to God in limiting Him and His Heavenly realms to my skewed perspective.

It has been my privilege to read Rachel's Heaven encounters. My own understanding has been enlightened and my heart set free inside a simple, yet deeper level of revelation of the love of God. I'm incredibly thankful to have been part of this project.

Jesus said, "Let the little children come to me, and do not hinder them, for the Kingdom of Heaven belongs to such as these" (Matthew 19:14). As Rachel teaches us about the Kingdom of God in Heaven and it's connection to earth, I'm desperately willing to learn of Him, whom my soul loves and longs for above all else. I hope you are too.

More Heaven Visits

There have been Heavenly encounters through the ages. Probably many, many more than we know about. There are many who have visited Heaven in our life-time. Some have shared their stories on TV, audio, video, and in books. Some have been on best-sellers' lists.

But, of course, Rachel knew nothing about them. Yet each one that tells about a genuine heaven experience seems to compliment another. We thank God for opening the Heavens for us all. Listed are several that we have read or listened to their stories.

Marietta Davis. . Scenes Beyond the Grave
Rebecca Springer. . Within the Gates
Ian McCormick. . A Glimpse of Eternity
Jesse Duplantis. . Heaven--Close Encounters of the God-kind
Don Piper. . 90 Minutes in Heaven
4-yr-old Victoria. . 6 BIG, BIG, BIG Angels
Marvin Bateman, Bank Pres.. . My Journey to Heaven
Colton Burpo, 3-yr-old. . Heaven is for Real
Dr. Mary C. Neal. . To Heaven and Back
Christopher Carter. . In the Palaces of Heaven

CHRISTOPHER CARTER:

We're here so that you can discover the Heavenly places right NOW. It is possible to see and live in that dimension. I've been encouraged these last few years by how many people are talking about their Heavenly encounters, and how many books are written about this topic.

My prayer is that perceiving, and interacting with the Heavenly realm will become as normal for you as reading your Bible. And, I pray that there will be a whole generation of believers who are as connected and conscious of the Heavens as they are the earth.

After reading through the testimonies, you'll be invited to start your own journey into the Heavenly places. And I can help you with that. I believe that this is for everyone.

Marvin Bateman:

At seventy-one, I had just had surgery at the University of Michigan Medical Center to remove a rare pancreatic tumor called insulinoma, racked with pain, I just wanted to sleep. I had no idea I was about to get an escape beyond my wildest dreams.

It's truly a place that is everything good and beautiful you can imagine, where you will feel more free and loved than you ever dreamed possible. It's really a future to eagerly await. .

I just couldn't stop thinking about my angels, and the radiant and peaceful place called Heaven I flew to with them. Images from that journey bombarded me: the color-bursts that lit up the sky, the hundreds and thousands of babies and children I saw, and for one twinkly in time, the glimpse I had of God's throne with two indescribable images upon it.

In the end, everyone who sees Heaven even for one second wants to stay forever, no matter how nice their life might be here on earth.

Dr. Mary:

While boating, I was pinned underwater in my kayak and drowned. I died and went to Heaven. After a brief stay, I was returned to my body.

The series of events surrounding my accident and recovery were nothing short of miraculous. Not only did I have the privilege of experiencing Heaven, but I continued to experience the intensity of God's world and conversed with angels several times in the weeks after my return.

Through this experience and conversation, I gained an understanding of many of life's important questions, such as "What happens when we die?" "Why are we here?" and "Why do bad things happen to good people?" I also gained an understanding of the disciple Paul's statement from I Corinthians 13 that of faith, hope, and love, the most enduring is love. I already had reasons to believe in miracles, but taking a journey to Heaven and back transformed my faith into knowledge and my hope into reality. My love remained unchanged and everlasting.

Ian McCormack:

Ian was night diving off the island of Mauritius when he was stung multiple times by Box Jellyfish, which are among the most venomous creatures in the world. His testimony relates how he clung to life while getting to hospital, was declared clinically dead soon afterwards, and how during this time, he had an encounter with Jesus, which radically changed the direction of his life.

During this time he experienced hell and Heaven and came back to tell the story! Dying was his doorway to true life and his story is still transforming lives around the world as it touches on some of the deepest questions we all eventually ask.

FRANCIS FRANGIPANE:

. . do not accept that God has permanently hidden Himself from you, though during trials it may seem so. He is teaching us to see in the dark and to hear in the silence. He is making Himself known to our inner man so that, regardless of outer circumstances, we can continually be led by His Spirit.

"He said, "They're future books. They will be made on earth later."
I looked in one book. It had a picture of me on
every page—the same picture with words under it. "

~~~~~~~~~~

This was taken from the last dream recorded in this journal.
How appropriate that this first portion of dreams ends talking about
Rachel's future first book—this one!"

Introducing God's Lil People Series!

These are true stories of children's miracles, written for little people. You'll love the illustrations too, all done by little people! Producing children's books was new adventure for me! Reaching little people around the world with the Love of Papa God is a growing passion! —Mama G—

Check the website for books and new translations as they become available. *Heaven Now* is also available on the websites: www.godslilpeople.com and www.destinymin.com. Also on Kindle and Amazon.

DESTINY MINISTRIES INT'L

Lou and Thelma Goszleth and Danny and Shana Orser work together from home base in Kissimmee, Florida. We are a network ministry, linked with many other ministries and missions: www.destinymin.com

THANK YOU

To June Taylor, for painting the Heavenly cover for Rachel's book. Rachel was very happy with it! Thanks a bunch, Sis. —reflectionsbyjtaylor.com

To Diane Connis, for taking everything I send you, and artistically putting it together to make a masterpiece. Your long hours and abilities at the computer never cease to amaze me. Thank you, my dear friend. —aplacecalledspecial.com

To Five Stones Publishing. Thank you, Randy and Coral for your help all the way through these projects. Now, on to other translations—at your recommendation. We couldn't have done it without you! Randall Johnson, International Publishing Consultant —www.ilncenter.com

Lightning Source UK Ltd.
Milton Keynes UK
UKHW051822130319
339097UK00005B/174/P